Chicken

MAGIC
In Minutes

Publications International, Ltd.

Favorite Brand Name Recipes at www.fbnr.com

Pictured on the front cover: Spicy Mango Chicken *(page 132)*.

Pictured on the back cover *(counterclockwise from top left):* Classic Family Lasagna *(page 28)*, Chicken Jambalaya *(page 40)* and Southern BBQ Chicken and Rice *(page 96)*.

ISBN: 0-7853-9118-5

Library of Congress Control Number: 2002117326

Manufactured in China.

8 7 6 5 4 3 2 1

Microwave Cooking: Microwave ovens vary in wattage. Use the cooking times as guidelines and check for doneness before adding more time.

Preparation/Cooking Times: Preparation times are based on the approximate amount of time required to assemble the recipe before cooking, baking, chilling or serving. These times include preparation steps such as measuring, chopping and mixing. The fact that some preparations and cooking can be done simultaneously is taken into account. Preparation of optional ingredients and serving suggestions is not included.

Contents

p. 66

p. 72

p. 110

Shopping Tips

• Look for secure, unbroken packaging, as well as a "sell-by" date that indicates the last day the chicken should be sold.

• Inspect the chicken. The skin should be creamy white to deep yellow. (Skin color is dependent on the chicken's diet.) The chicken should be plump, and the meat should never look gray or pasty.

• Odors signal spoilage. If you notice a strong, unpleasant odor after opening a package of chicken, return the chicken in its original packaging to the store for a refund.

• Two whole chicken breasts yield about two cups chopped cooked chicken; one broiler-fryer (about three pounds) yields about two and one-half cups chopped cooked chicken.

Storing

• Raw chicken is very perishable and must be handled with care. Buy it just before returning home and refrigerate it as soon as possible.

• Fresh raw chicken can be stored in its original packaging for up to two days in the coldest part of the refrigerator.

• Freeze chicken immediately if you do not plan to use it within two days after purchasing. You can freeze raw chicken tightly wrapped in plastic wrap, freezer paper or foil for up to one year. Airtight packaging, the key to freezing chicken successfully, prevents ice crystals from forming.

• When freezing whole chickens, remove and rinse the giblets (if any) and pat dry with paper towels. Rinse and dry the chicken and trim away any excess fat. Tightly wrap, label, date and freeze the chicken and giblets separately in plastic wrap, freezer paper or foil. Giblets should be used within two to three months.

• Consider wrapping chicken pieces individually in plastic wrap, then placing them in a resealable freezer bag before freezing. This will allow you to remove and thaw only the amount you need. Plus, individual pieces thaw quicker.

• **DO NOT** allow other food to come in contact with a thawing chicken or its juices.

• Cooked chicken can be frozen for up to two months.

Handling

Raw chicken can contain salmonella bacteria, but with careful handling and proper cooking methods, you can eliminate any health concerns. Follow these helpful tips:

• Raw chicken should be rinsed and patted dry with paper towels before cooking. Cutting boards and knives must be washed in hot sudsy water after use and before being reused for any other food preparation. Always wash your hands thoroughly before and after handling raw chicken.

• **DO NOT** thaw frozen chicken on the kitchen counter, since bacteria grow more quickly at room temperature. Instead, thaw it, wrapped, in the refrigerator. Allow at least 24 hours of thawing time for a 5-pound whole chicken, and five hours per pound of chicken pieces. Never refreeze chicken that has been thawed.

• Always cook chicken completely. **DO NOT** partially cook it, and store it to be completely cooked later.

• When stuffing a chicken, lightly stuff the cavity just before cooking. **DO NOT** stuff it in advance.

• Chicken should be eaten, refrigerated or frozen within two hours of cooking.

Is It Done Yet?

- **Whole chickens:** A meat thermometer inserted into the thickest part of the thigh, not touching bone or fat, should register 180°F before the chicken is removed from the oven.

- **Stuffed whole chickens:** A meat thermometer inserted into the center of the stuffing inside the body cavity should register 165°F.

- **Whole chicken breasts:** A meat thermometer inserted into the thickest part of the breast should register 170°F.

- **Bone-in chicken pieces:** You should be able to easily insert a fork into the chicken, and the juices should run clear when the pieces are completely cooked. However, the meat and juices nearest the bone might still be pink even though the chicken is completely cooked.

- **Boneless chicken pieces:** The chicken piece should no longer be pink in the center. To check, just cut into it with a knife.

Cooking Methods

- **Sautéing** is a quick-cooking method. Chicken pieces are browned and turned frequently in a small amount of oil or fat over medium to medium-high heat. Thin cuts, such as boneless chicken breasts, cook completely during browning. For thicker pieces, reduce the heat, cover and cook gently until the chicken is no longer pink in the center. Sautéing promotes even cooking and produces a crisp, brown surface that locks in flavorful juices. It is an ideal way to cook boneless, skinless chicken breasts.

- **Pan-frying** is a quick-cooking method in which chicken pieces are typically coated with seasoned flour or bread crumbs and cooked in a skillet in approximately one-half inch of hot vegetable oil or fat over medium to medium-high heat.

- **Deep-frying** is the method of submerging chicken pieces coated with seasoned flour or batter in hot vegetable oil or fat.

- **Braising** is a two-step cooking method. Chicken pieces are first browned in a small amount of fat (sautéed), then covered and slowly cooked in a small amount of liquid over low heat. During the slow-cooking stage, the chicken flavors combine with the other ingredients, resulting in tender, tasty meat.

- **Poaching** is the method of gently simmering chicken pieces in a liquid. Meat from poached chicken is tender, juicy and mild in flavor and is often used in salads, casseroles, sandwiches and recipes calling for cooked chicken.

- **Roasting** is the dry-heat method of cooking a whole chicken (uncovered) in the oven. It results in a well-browned exterior and a moist and tender interior. To prepare a whole chicken for roasting, remove the giblets from the chicken cavity and discard or reserve them for another use. Rinse the chicken under cold water and pat it dry with paper towels. Insert a meat thermometer into the center of the thickest part of the thigh, not touching bone. Tuck the wings under the back and tie the legs together with wet cotton string. Place the chicken breast-side-up on the rack inside the roasting pan. Prevent the chicken from drying out by basting it with pan juices every 10 to 15 minutes. When the chicken has reached the proper temperature, remove it from the oven, loosely cover it with foil and let it stand 10 to 15 minutes before carving.

- **Broiling** is done by cooking chicken pieces four to six inches above or below the heat source in an oven or on a range-top grill. The chicken is cooked on both sides until the outside is browned and the inside is moist and tender. Broiling can dry out chicken. Avoid this by either marinating the chicken before broiling, or brushing it with oil, butter or a flavorful sauce during broiling.

- **Grilling** is done by cooking chicken pieces on a grill grid directly over hot coals. A single layer of charcoal should extend one to two inches beyond the cooking area of the food.

One-Dish Wonders

Broccoli, Chicken and Rice Casserole

1 box UNCLE BEN'S CHEF'S RECIPE™ Broccoli Rice Au Gratin Supreme
2 cups boiling water
4 boneless, skinless chicken breasts (about 1 pound)
¼ teaspoon garlic powder
2 cups frozen broccoli
1 cup (4 ounces) reduced-fat shredded Cheddar cheese

1. Heat oven to 425°F. In 13×9-inch baking pan, combine rice and contents of seasoning packet. Add boiling water; mix well. Add chicken; sprinkle with garlic powder. Cover and bake 30 minutes.

2. Add broccoli and cheese; continue to bake, covered, 8 to 10 minutes or until chicken is no longer pink in center. *Makes 4 servings*

Broccoli, Chicken and Rice Casserole

Chicken Enchiladas

2 cups chopped cooked
  chicken or turkey
1 cup chopped green
  pepper
1 package (8 ounces)
  PHILADELPHIA® Cream
  Cheese, cubed
1 cup TACO BELL® HOME
  ORIGINALS®* Thick 'N
  Chunky Salsa, divided
8 (6-inch) flour tortillas
¾ pound (12 ounces)
  VELVEETA® Pasteurized
  Prepared Cheese
  Product, cut up
¼ cup milk

*TACO BELL and HOME ORIGINALS
are registered trademarks owned and
licensed by Taco Bell Corp.

MIX chicken, green pepper, cream cheese and ½ cup of the salsa in saucepan, stirring occasionally; cook over low heat until cream cheese is melted.

SPOON ⅓ cup chicken mixture down center of each tortilla; roll up. Place, seam-side down, in lightly greased 12×8-inch baking dish.

MIX prepared cheese product and milk in saucepan; cook over low heat until prepared cheese product is completely melted, stirring frequently. Pour over enchiladas; cover with foil.

BAKE at 350°F for 20 minutes or until thoroughly heated. Top with remaining salsa.

Makes 4 to 6 servings

Prep: 20 minutes
Bake: 20 minutes

Bayou Chicken Bake

4 to 6 PERDUE®
  Individually Frozen™
  boneless, skinless
  chicken breasts
1½ to 2 teaspoons Cajun or
  Creole seasoning
2 cans (14½ ounces each)
  Cajun-style stewed
  tomatoes
1 package (16 ounces)
  frozen black-eyed peas
1 cup uncooked regular
  long-grain rice
½ cup chopped onion
2 tablespoons chopped
  fresh parsley

Preheat oven to 350°F. Lightly grease 13×9-inch baking dish. Sprinkle chicken with Cajun seasoning; place in baking dish. In large bowl, combine tomatoes, black-eyed peas, rice and onion. Pour over chicken. Cover and bake 45 minutes. Uncover and bake 15 minutes longer, or until chicken is cooked through. Sprinkle with parsley before serving. *Makes 4 to 6 servings*

Chicken Enchiladas

Savory Chicken and Biscuits

1 pound boneless, skinless chicken thighs or breasts, cut into 1-inch pieces

1 medium potato, cut into 1-inch pieces

1 medium yellow onion, cut into 1-inch pieces

8 ounces fresh mushrooms, quartered

1 cup fresh baby carrots

1 cup chopped celery

1 ($14\frac{1}{2}$-ounce) can chicken broth

3 cloves garlic, minced

1 teaspoon dried rosemary leaves

1 teaspoon salt

1 teaspoon black pepper

3 tablespoons cornstarch blended with $\frac{1}{2}$ cup cold water

1 cup frozen peas, thawed

1 (4-ounce) jar sliced pimientos, drained

1 package BOB EVANS® Frozen Buttermilk Biscuit Dough

Preheat oven to 375°F. Combine chicken, potato, onion, mushrooms, carrots, celery, broth, garlic, rosemary, salt and pepper in large saucepan. Bring to a boil over high heat. Reduce heat to low and simmer, uncovered, 5 minutes. Stir in cornstarch mixture; cook 2 minutes. Stir in peas and pimientos; return to a boil. Transfer chicken mixture to 2-quart casserole dish; arrange frozen biscuits on top. Bake 30 to 35 minutes or until biscuits are golden brown. Refrigerate leftovers.

Makes 4 to 6 servings

Magical Tip

Chopping is the technique of cutting food into small, irregularly shaped pieces. Although the term does not imply a specific size, most cooks would suggest food be chopped into approximately one-quarter-inch pieces.

Savory Chicken and Biscuits

Chicken Mexicana Casserole

10 boneless, skinless chicken breasts, (about 2½ pounds) cut into 1-inch cubes

2 packages (1.0 ounce each) LAWRY'S® Taco Spices & Seasonings

2 cans (14½ ounces each) whole tomatoes, undrained; cut up

3 cups (12 ounces) shredded sharp Cheddar cheese, divided

1 can (7 ounces) diced green chiles, undrained

1 can (12 ounces) whole kernel corn, drained

1 package (8¼ ounces) corn muffin mix

2 eggs

¼ cup sour cream

In large bowl, toss chicken cubes with Taco Spices & Seasonings and tomatoes; mix well. Add 1 cup cheese. Spread mixture evenly into 13×9×2-inch baking dish. Spoon chiles over chicken mixture; sprinkle with remaining cheese. Set aside. In medium bowl, combine remaining ingredients; mix well. Drop by rounded spoonfuls on top of casserole, spacing evenly. Bake in 350°F oven 50 to 60 minutes or until top is lightly browned and sauce is bubbly. Remove from oven and let stand about 20 minutes before serving.   *Makes 10 to 12 servings*

Serving Suggestion: Serve with black beans and sliced tomatoes.

Chicken Mexicana Casserole

Mini Chicken Pot Pies

1 container (about
   16 ounces)
   refrigerated reduced-
   fat buttermilk biscuits
1½ cups milk
1 package (1.8 ounces)
   white sauce mix
2 cups cut-up cooked
   chicken
1 cup frozen assorted
   vegetables, partially
   thawed
2 cups shredded Cheddar
   cheese
2 cups French's® Taste
   Toppers™ French Fried
   Onions

1. Preheat oven to 400°F. Separate biscuits; press into 8 (8-ounce) custard cups, pressing up sides to form crust.

2. Whisk milk and sauce mix in medium saucepan. Bring to boiling over medium-high heat. Reduce heat to medium-low; simmer 1 minute, whisking constantly, until thickened. Stir in chicken and vegetables.

3. Spoon about ⅓ cup chicken mixture into each crust. Place cups on baking sheet. Bake 15 minutes or until golden brown. Top each with cheese and *Taste Toppers*. Bake 3 minutes or until golden. To serve, remove from cups and transfer to serving plates. *Makes 8 servings*

Prep Time: 15 minutes
Cook Time: about 20 minutes

Country Chicken Dinner

¼ cup milk
2 tablespoons margarine or
   butter
1 package (4.7 ounces)
   PASTA RONI® Chicken
   & Broccoli Flavor with
   Linguine
2 cups frozen mixed
   broccoli, cauliflower
   and carrots vegetable
   medley
2 cups chopped cooked
   chicken or turkey
1 teaspoon dried basil
   leaves

1. In round 3-quart microwavable glass casserole, combine 1¾ cups water, milk and margarine. Microwave, uncovered, at HIGH 4 to 5 minutes or until boiling.

2. Gradually add pasta while stirring.

3. Stir in Special Seasonings, frozen vegetables, chicken and basil.

4. Microwave, uncovered, at HIGH 14 to 15 minutes, stirring gently after 7 minutes. Sauce will be thin, but will thicken upon standing.

5. Let stand 4 to 5 minutes or until desired consistency. Stir before serving. *Makes 4 servings*

Mini Chicken Pot Pies

Chicken Fajita Casserole

One-Dish Wonders

8 TYSON® Fresh Chicken Breast Tenders or Individually Fresh Frozen® Boneless, Skinless Chicken Tenderloins

1 box UNCLE BEN'S CHEF'S RECIPE™ Traditional Red Beans & Rice

1 can (4 ounces) sliced black olives, drained

1 can (4 ounces) diced green chilies, drained

2 cups boiling water

1 can (15 ounces) diced tomatoes

1 cup (4 ounces) shredded Monterey Jack cheese

1 cup crushed tortilla chips

PREP: Preheat oven to 350°F. CLEAN: Wash hands. Remove protective ice glaze from frozen chicken by holding under cool running water 1 to 2 minutes. Place red beans and rice (do not include seasoning packet) in 13×9-inch baking dish; top with olives and chilies. Place chicken in baking dish. CLEAN: Wash hands. In medium bowl, combine boiling water, tomatoes and contents of rice seasoning packet. Pour over chicken mixture.

COOK: Cover and bake 45 minutes. Remove cover; sprinkle with cheese and tortilla chips. Bake 5 minutes or until rice is cooked and internal juices of chicken run clear. (Or insert instant-read meat thermometer in thickest part of chicken. Temperature should read 170°F.)

SERVE: Serve with a tossed salad and lemon sherbet, if desired.

CHILL: Refrigerate leftovers immediately.

Makes 4 servings

Prep Time: 10 minutes
Cook Time: 50 minutes

Scalloped Chicken & Pasta

¼ cup margarine or butter, divided

1 package (6.2 ounces) PASTA RONI® Shells & White Cheddar

2 cups frozen mixed vegetables

⅔ cup milk

2 cups chopped cooked chicken or ham

¼ cup dry bread crumbs

1. Preheat oven to 450°F.

2. In 3-quart saucepan, combine 2¼ cups water and 2 tablespoons margarine. Bring just to a boil. Stir in pasta and frozen vegetables. Reduce heat to medium.

3. Boil, uncovered, stirring frequently, 12 to 14 minutes or until most of water is absorbed. Add Special Seasonings, milk and chicken. Continue cooking 3 minutes.

4. Meanwhile, melt remaining 2 tablespoons margarine in small saucepan; stir in bread crumbs.

5. Transfer pasta mixture to 8- or 9-inch square glass baking dish. Sprinkle with bread crumb mixture. Bake 10 minutes or until bread crumbs are browned and edges are bubbly. *Makes 4 servings*

Fettuccine with Chicken Breasts

12 ounces uncooked fettuccine or egg noodles

1 cup HIDDEN VALLEY® Original Ranch® Dressing

⅓ cup Dijon mustard

8 boneless, skinless chicken breast halves, pounded thin

½ cup butter

⅓ cup dry white wine

Cook fettuccine according to package directions; drain. Preheat oven to 425°F. Stir together dressing and mustard; set aside. Pour fettuccine into oiled baking dish. Sauté chicken in butter in a large skillet until no longer pink in center. Transfer cooked chicken to the bed of fettuccine. Add wine to the skillet; cook until reduced to desired consistency. Drizzle over chicken. Pour the reserved dressing mixture over the chicken. Bake at 425°F. about 10 minutes, or until dressing forms a golden brown crust. *Makes 8 servings*

Sweet & Sour Chicken and Rice

One-Dish Wonders

1 pound chicken tenders

1 can (8 ounces) pineapple chunks, drained and juice reserved

1 cup uncooked rice

2 carrots, thinly sliced

1 green bell pepper, cut into 1-inch pieces

1 large onion, chopped

3 cloves garlic, minced

1 can (14½ ounces) reduced-sodium chicken broth

⅓ cup soy sauce

3 tablespoons sugar

3 tablespoons apple cider vinegar

1 tablespoon sesame oil

1½ teaspoons ground ginger

¼ cup chopped peanuts (optional)

Chopped fresh cilantro (optional)

Preheat oven to 350°F. Spray 13×9-inch baking dish with nonstick cooking spray.

Combine chicken, pineapple chunks, rice, carrots, pepper, onion and garlic in prepared dish.

Place broth, reserved pineapple juice, soy sauce, sugar, vinegar, sesame oil and ginger in small saucepan; bring to a boil over high heat. Remove from heat and pour over chicken mixture.

Cover tightly with foil and bake 40 to 50 minutes or until chicken is no longer pink in centers and rice is tender. Sprinkle with peanuts and cilantro, if desired.

Makes 6 servings

Magical Tip

Chicken "tenders," or "supremes," are the lean, tender strips found on the underside of the breast. They are skinless and boneless and have virtually no waste.

Chicken in French Onion Sauce

1 package (10 ounces) frozen baby carrots, thawed and drained, or 4 medium carrots, cut into strips (about 2 cups)

2 cups sliced mushrooms

½ cup thinly sliced celery

1⅓ cups *French's® Taste Toppers*™ French Fried Onions, divided

4 chicken breast halves, skinned and boned

½ cup white wine

¾ cup prepared chicken bouillon

½ teaspoon garlic salt

½ teaspoon pepper

Paprika

Preheat oven to 375°F. In 12×8-inch baking dish, combine vegetables and ⅔ *cup* **Taste Toppers**. Arrange chicken breasts on vegetables. In small bowl, combine wine, bouillon, garlic salt and pepper; pour over chicken and vegetables. Sprinkle chicken with paprika. Bake, covered, at 375°F for 35 minutes or until chicken is done. Baste chicken with wine sauce and top with remaining ⅔ *cup* **Taste Toppers;** bake, uncovered, 3 minutes or until **Taste Toppers** are golden brown.

Makes 4 servings

Microwave Directions: In 8×12-inch microwave-safe dish, combine vegetables and ⅔ *cup* onions. Arrange chicken breasts, skinned side down, along sides of dish. Prepare wine mixture as above, except reduce bouillon to ⅓ cup; pour over chicken and vegetables. Cook, covered, on HIGH 6 minutes. Turn chicken breasts over and sprinkle with paprika. Stir vegetables and rotate dish. Cook, covered, 7 to 9 minutes or until chicken is done. Baste chicken with wine sauce and top with remaining ⅔ *cup* onions; cook, uncovered, 1 minute. Let stand 5 minutes.

Chicken in French Onion Sauce

Creamy Chicken and Pasta with Spinach

6 ounces uncooked egg noodles

1 tablespoon olive oil

¼ cup chopped onion

¼ cup chopped red bell pepper

1 package (10 ounces) frozen spinach, thawed and drained

2 boneless skinless chicken breast halves (¾ pound), cooked and cut into 1-inch pieces

1 can (4 ounces) sliced mushrooms, drained

2 cups (8 ounces) shredded Swiss cheese

1 container (8 ounces) sour cream

¾ cup half-and-half

2 eggs, slightly beaten

½ teaspoon salt

Red onion and fresh spinach for garnish

Preheat oven to 350°F. Prepare egg noodles according to package directions; set aside.

Heat oil in large skillet over medium-high heat. Add onion and bell pepper; cook and stir 2 minutes or until onion is tender. Add spinach, chicken, mushrooms and cooked noodles; stir to combine.

Combine cheese, sour cream, half-and-half, eggs and salt in medium bowl; blend well.

Add cheese mixture to chicken mixture; stir to combine. Pour into 13×9-inch baking dish coated with nonstick cooking spray. Bake, covered, 30 to 35 minutes or until heated through. Garnish with red onion and fresh spinach, if desired. *Makes 8 servings*

Magical Tip

The green bell pepper, known for its bell-like shape, is picked before it ripens. When ripened, the pepper turns red, yellow, orange, white or purple, depending on the variety.

Creamy Chicken and Pasta with Spinach

Tortilla Chicken Bake

1 can (14½ ounces) DEL MONTE® Mexican Recipe Stewed Tomatoes

½ cup chopped onion

2 cloves garlic, crushed

½ teaspoon dried oregano, crushed

½ teaspoon chili powder

½ pound boneless chicken, skinned and cut into strips

4 cups tortilla chips

¾ cup shredded Monterey Jack cheese with jalapeño peppers or Cheddar cheese

1. Preheat oven to 375°F. Drain tomatoes, reserving liquid; chop tomatoes.

2. Combine reserved liquid, onion, garlic, oregano and chili powder in large skillet; boil 5 minutes, stirring occasionally.

3. Stir in tomatoes and chicken; cook over medium heat until chicken is no longer pink, about 3 minutes. Layer half of chips, chicken mixture and cheese in shallow 2-quart baking dish; repeat layers, ending with cheese.

4. Cover and bake 15 minutes or until heated through. Serve with sour cream, if desired.   *Makes 4 servings*

Prep Time: 3 minutes
Cook Time: 25 minutes

The Original Ranch® Tetrazzini

8 ounces linguine, cooked and drained

3 cups shredded cooked chicken

1½ cups prepared HIDDEN VALLEY® The Original Ranch® Salad Dressing

½ cup dry white wine or chicken broth

1 jar (4½ ounces) sliced mushrooms, drained

¼ cup buttered* bread crumbs

Combine linguine, chicken, dressing, wine and mushrooms. Pour into a 2-quart casserole dish. Top with crumbs. Bake at 350°F. for 20 minutes or until bubbly around edges.   *Makes 6 servings*

*Melt 1½ teaspoons butter; stir in plain dry bread crumbs until evenly coated.

Pennsylvania Dutch Chicken Bake

1 package (about
    1¾ pounds) PERDUE®
    Fresh Skinless Chicken
    Thighs

  Salt and pepper to taste

1 to 2 tablespoons canola
    oil

1 can (14 to 16 ounces)
    sauerkraut, undrained

1 can (14 to 15 ounces)
    whole onions, drained

1 tart red apple, unpeeled,
    sliced

6 to 8 dried whole apricots

½ cup raisins

¼ cup brown sugar, or to
    taste

Preheat oven to 350°F. Season thighs with salt and pepper. In large nonstick skillet over medium-high heat, heat oil. Cook thighs 6 to 8 minutes per side until browned. Meanwhile, in 12×9-inch shallow baking dish, mix sauerkraut, onions, apple, apricots, raisins and brown sugar until blended. Arrange thighs in sauerkraut mixture. Cover and bake 30 to 40 minutes or until chicken is cooked through and a meat thermometer inserted in thickest part of thigh registers 180°F.

Makes 6 servings

Tip: If desired, substitute other fresh or dried fruit in this recipe, such as pears or pitted prunes.

One-Dish Chicken Florentine

4 boneless, skinless
    chicken breast halves
    (about 1¼ pounds)

1 jar (26 to 28 ounces)
    RAGÚ® Old World Style®
    Pasta Sauce

1½ cups water

1¼ cups uncooked regular or
    converted rice

1 package (10 ounces)
    frozen chopped
    spinach, thawed

1 cup shredded mozzarella
    cheese (about
    4 ounces)

1. Preheat oven to 375°F. Season chicken, if desired, with salt and pepper.

2. In 13×9-inch baking dish, combine Ragú Pasta Sauce, water, rice and spinach. Arrange chicken on uncooked rice mixture.

3. Bake uncovered 30 minutes. Sprinkle with cheese and bake an additional 10 minutes or until chicken is no longer pink. Let stand 10 minutes before serving.

Makes 4 servings

Prep Time: 5 minutes
Cook Time: 40 minutes

Chicken & Rice Bake

1 can (10¾ ounces) condensed cream of mushroom soup

1¾ cups water

¾ cup uncooked long-grain rice

1½ cups sliced mushrooms

1⅓ cups *French's®* *Taste Toppers*™ French Fried Onions, divided

4 teaspoons *French's®* Worcestershire Sauce, divided

4 chicken breast halves (about 2 pounds)

½ teaspoon *each* paprika and dried thyme leaves

Preheat oven to 375°F. Combine soup, water, rice, mushrooms, ⅔ cup **Taste Toppers** and 2 teaspoons Worcestershire in 3-quart oblong baking dish. Arrange chicken over rice mixture. Brush chicken with remaining Worcestershire and sprinkle with paprika and thyme.

Bake, uncovered, 1 hour or until chicken is no longer pink in center. Top with remaining ⅔ cup **Taste Toppers**. Bake 3 minutes or until **Taste Toppers** are golden.   *Makes 4 servings*

Tip: Remove skin from chicken before baking, if desired.

Prep Time: 10 minutes
Cook Time: about 1 hour

Swiss 'n' Chicken Casserole

4 cups chopped cooked chicken

2 cups KRAFT® Shredded Swiss Cheese

2 cups croutons

2 cups sliced celery

1 cup MIRACLE WHIP® or MIRACLE WHIP® LIGHT Dressing

½ cup milk

¼ cup chopped onion

Chopped walnuts (optional)

• Heat oven to 350°F.

• Mix all ingredients. Spoon into 2-quart casserole. Sprinkle with walnuts, if desired.

• Bake 40 minutes or until thoroughly heated.
Makes 6 servings

Prep Time: 20 minutes
Cook Time: 40 minutes

Chicken & Rice Bake

Classic Family Lasagna

One-Dish Wonders

1 package (1 pound) TYSON® Fresh Ground Chicken

9 lasagna noodles, cooked according to package directions

1 medium onion, chopped

½ cup chopped green bell pepper (optional)

2 cloves garlic, minced

1 jar (30 ounces) spaghetti sauce

1 container (15 ounces) ricotta cheese

¾ cup grated Parmesan cheese, divided

1 egg, beaten

¼ teaspoon black pepper

3½ cups (14 ounces) shredded mozzarella cheese

PREP: Preheat oven to 375°F. CLEAN: Wash hands. In large skillet, cook and stir chicken, onion, bell pepper and garlic over medium-high heat until chicken is no longer pink. Stir in sauce; heat through and set aside. In medium bowl, combine ricotta cheese, ½ cup Parmesan cheese, egg and black pepper; mix well. Spray 13×9-inch baking dish with nonstick cooking spray. Spread ⅓ cup sauce on bottom of dish. Top with 3 noodles, one-third of sauce, one-third of ricotta mixture and 1 cup mozzarella cheese. Repeat layers twice, except do not top with remaining 1½ cups mozzarella cheese. Cover tightly with foil sprayed lightly with nonstick cooking spray.

COOK: Bake 40 minutes. Remove foil. Top with remaining cheese. Bake 15 minutes or until bubbly and cheese is melted.

SERVE: Serve with a green salad and garlic bread, if desired.

SERVE: Refrigerate leftovers immediately.

Makes 12 servings

Prep Time: 35 minutes
Cook Time: about 1 hour

Classic Family Lasagna

Home-Style Chicken 'n Biscuits

5 slices bacon, fried crisp and crumbled

1½ cups (7 ounces) cubed cooked chicken

1 package (10 ounces) frozen mixed vegetables, thawed and drained

1½ cups (6 ounces) shredded Cheddar cheese

2 medium tomatoes, chopped (about 1 cup)

1 can (10¾ ounces) condensed cream of chicken soup

¾ cup milk

1½ cups biscuit baking mix

⅔ cup milk

1⅓ cups *French's*® *Taste Toppers*™ French Fried Onions, divided

Preheat oven to 400°F. In large bowl, combine bacon, chicken, mixed vegetables, *1 cup* cheese, tomatoes, soup and ¾ cup milk. Pour chicken mixture into greased 12×8-inch baking dish. Bake, covered, at 400°F for 15 minutes. Meanwhile, in medium bowl, combine baking mix, ⅔ cup milk and ⅔ *cup* **Taste Toppers** to form soft dough. Spoon biscuit dough in 6 mounds around edges of casserole. Bake, uncovered, 15 to 20 minutes or until biscuits are golden brown. Top biscuits with remaining cheese and ⅔ *cup* **Taste Toppers;** bake 1 to 3 minutes or until **Taste Toppers** are golden brown.
Makes 6 servings

Microwave Directions: Prepare chicken mixture as directed, except reduce ¾ cup milk to ½ cup; pour into 12×8-inch microwave-safe dish. Cook, covered, on HIGH 10 minutes or until heated through. Stir chicken mixture halfway through cooking time. Prepare biscuit dough as directed. Stir casserole and spoon biscuit dough over hot chicken mixture as directed. Cook, uncovered, 7 to 8 minutes or until biscuits are done. Rotate dish halfway through cooking time. Top biscuits with remaining cheese and ⅔ *cup* onions; cook, uncovered, 1 minute or until cheese melts. Let stand 5 minutes.

Home-Style Chicken 'n Biscuits

Classic Fried Chicken

¾ cup all-purpose flour

1 teaspoon salt

¼ teaspoon pepper

1 frying chicken (2 ½ to 3 pounds), cut up, or chicken pieces

½ cup CRISCO® Oil*

*Use your favorite Crisco Oil product.

1. Combine flour, salt and pepper in paper or plastic bag. Add a few pieces of chicken at a time. Shake to coat.

2. Heat oil to 365°F in electric skillet or on medium-high heat in large heavy skillet. Fry chicken 30 to 40 minutes without lowering heat. Turn once for even browning. Drain on paper towels.   *Makes 4 servings*

Note: For thicker crust, increase flour to 1 ½ cups. Shake damp chicken in seasoned flour. Place on waxed paper. Let stand for 5 to 20 minutes before frying.

Spicy Fried Chicken: Increase pepper to ½ teaspoon. Combine pepper with ½ teaspoon poultry seasoning, ½ teaspoon paprika, ½ teaspoon cayenne pepper and ¼ teaspoon dry mustard. Rub on chicken before step 1. Substitute 2 ¼ teaspoons garlic salt, ¼ teaspoon salt and ¼ teaspoon celery salt for 1 teaspoon salt. Combine with flour in step 1 and proceed as directed above.

Classic Fried Chicken

Grilled Chicken Caesar Salad

8 cups torn romaine lettuce

1 pound boneless skinless chicken breasts, grilled, cut into strips

1 cup seasoned croutons

½ cup KRAFT® Shredded or 100% Grated Parmesan Cheese

¾ cup KRAFT FREE® Caesar Italian Fat Free Dressing

TOSS lettuce, chicken, croutons and cheese in large salad bowl.

ADD dressing; toss to coat. Serve with fresh lemon wedges and fresh ground pepper, if desired.

Makes 4 servings

Variation: Prepare as directed, substituting 1 package (10 ounces) mixed or romaine salad greens.

Prep Time: 15 minutes plus marinating
Grill Time: 20 minutes

Chicken Carbonara

1 pound chicken tenders

1 jar (12 ounces) Alfredo sauce

1 cup milk

1⅓ cups *French's*® *Taste Toppers*™ French Fried Onions, divided

½ of a 10-ounce package frozen peas, thawed and drained

2 tablespoons real bacon bits*

Hot cooked pasta

*Or, substitute 2 strips crumbled, cooked bacon for real bacon bits.

Spray large nonstick skillet with nonstick cooking spray; heat over high heat. Add chicken; cook and stir about 5 minutes or until browned.

Stir in Alfredo sauce and milk. Add ⅔ *cup* **Taste Toppers**, peas and bacon bits. Bring to a boil. Reduce heat to low. Cook 5 minutes, stirring occasionally. Serve over pasta. Sprinkle with remaining ⅔ *cup* **Taste Toppers**.

Makes 4 to 6 servings

Prep Time: 10 minutes
Cook Time: 10 minutes

Grilled Chicken Caesar Salad

Oven-Baked Chicken Parmesan

4 boneless, skinless
  chicken breast halves
  (about 1 ¼ pounds)
1 egg, slightly beaten
¾ cup Italian seasoned dry
  bread crumbs
1 jar (26 to 28 ounces)
  RAGÚ® Old World Style®
  Pasta Sauce
1 cup shredded mozzarella
  cheese (about
  4 ounces)

1. Preheat oven to 400°F. Dip chicken in egg, then bread crumbs, coating well.

2. In 13×9-inch glass baking dish, arrange chicken. Bake uncovered 20 minutes.

3. Pour Ragú Pasta Sauce over chicken, then top with cheese. Bake an additional 10 minutes or until chicken is no longer pink. Serve, if desired, with hot cooked pasta.   *Makes 4 servings*

Prep Time: 10 minutes
Cook Time: 30 minutes

Magical Tip

Chicken breasts are available whole, but are often split. Recipe references to chicken breasts usually mean a chicken breast half.

Oven-Baked Chicken Parmesan

Broccoli Cheese Casserole

3 whole chicken breasts, skinned and halved

1½ pounds fresh broccoli

2 tablespoons margarine

½ cup chopped onion

1 clove garlic, minced

3 tablespoons all-purpose flour

1¼ cups skim milk

2 tablespoons fresh parsley

½ teaspoon salt

½ teaspoon dried oregano leaves, crushed

1½ cups 1% low fat cream-style small curd cottage cheese

1½ cups shredded reduced fat Wisconsin Cheddar cheese

¼ cup grated Wisconsin Romano cheese

1 jar (4½ ounces) sliced mushrooms, drained

6 ounces noodles, cooked and drained

MICROWAVE DIRECTIONS

Place chicken breasts in microwavable glass baking dish. Microwave at HIGH (100% power) 7 minutes. Cool slightly and cube. Set aside. Remove flowerets from broccoli and cut larger ones in half. Cut stems into 1-inch pieces. Place broccoli in 3-quart microwavable baking dish with ½ cup water. Cover and microwave at HIGH (100% power) 7 minutes, stirring once. Let stand, covered, 2 minutes. Drain well; set aside.

Place margarine, onion and garlic in same baking dish. Cover and microwave at HIGH (100% power) 3 minutes. Stir in flour. Gradually add milk. Add parsley, salt and oregano. Microwave at HIGH (100% power) 1 minute. Stir well; microwave 1 minute. Stir in cottage cheese. Microwave at HIGH (100% power) 2 minutes. Stir; microwave 2 minutes. Add Cheddar and Romano cheeses, stirring well. Microwave at MEDIUM-HIGH (70% power) 2 minutes. Stir in chicken, broccoli, mushrooms and noodles. Cover and microwave at MEDIUM (50% power) 5 minutes or until heated through.   *Makes 6 to 8 servings*

*Favorite recipe from **Wisconsin Milk Marketing Board***

Light Chicken Cordon Bleu

½ cup seasoned dry bread crumbs

1 tablespoon grated Parmesan cheese

1 teaspoon chopped fresh parsley

½ teaspoon paprika

1 package (1 pound) PERDUE® FIT 'N EASY® Fresh Skinless and Boneless Oven Stuffer® Roaster Thin-Sliced Breast

1 package (6 ounces) reduced-fat Swiss cheese slices

1 package (6 ounces) turkey ham slices

1 egg white, beaten

MICROWAVE DIRECTIONS

In shallow bowl, combine first four ingredients. On each chicken breast slice, place 1 slice Swiss cheese and 2 overlapping slices ham; roll up, jelly-roll style, and secure with toothpick. Dip rolls in egg white, then coat with bread crumb mixture. In microwavable dish, arrange chicken rolls, seam sides down, in circular pattern. Cover with waxed paper; microwave at MEDIUM-HIGH (70% power) 5 minutes. Rearrange rolls; cover with double thickness of paper towels. Microwave at MEDIUM-HIGH 8 minutes. Let stand, uncovered, 5 to 10 minutes. *Makes 5 servings*

Magical Tip

Some recipes call for flattening chicken breasts so they can be filled and rolled or cooked more quickly. To flatten uncooked boneless chicken breasts, place one breast half between two sheets of waxed paper or plastic wrap. Using the flat side of a meat mallet or a rolling pin, gently pound the chicken from the center to the outside until the chicken is the desired thickness.

Chicken Jambalaya

2 tablespoons vegetable oil

¾ pound boneless chicken thighs or breasts, cut into cubes

1 cup ham cut into very thin strips (about 5 ounces)

1 can (14½ to 16 ounces) seasoned diced tomatoes in juice, undrained

1½ cups water

1 can (4 ounces) diced green chilies, undrained

1 package KNORR® Recipe Classics™ Vegetable Soup, Dip and Recipe Mix

1 cup uncooked rice

• In large skillet, heat oil over medium-high heat and brown chicken and ham.

• Stir in tomatoes, water, chilies and recipe mix. Bring to a boil over high heat. Stir in rice.

• Reduce heat to low and simmer covered, stirring occasionally, 20 minutes or until rice is tender.

Makes 4 servings

Prep Time: 15 minutes
Cook Time: 25 minutes

Chicken Jambalaya

Chicken Cacciatore

8 ounces noodles,
 uncooked

1 can (15 ounces) chunky
 Italian-style tomato
 sauce

1 cup chopped green bell
 pepper

1 cup sliced onion

1 cup sliced mushrooms

 Nonstick cooking spray

4 boneless skinless chicken
 breast halves
 (1 pound)

 Salt

 Black pepper

1. Cook noodles according to package directions; drain.

2. While noodles are cooking, combine tomato sauce, bell pepper, onion and mushrooms in microwavable dish. Cover loosely with plastic wrap or waxed paper; microwave at HIGH 6 to 8 minutes, stirring halfway through cooking time.

3. While sauce mixture is cooking, coat large skillet with cooking spray and heat over medium-high heat. Cook chicken breasts 3 to 4 minutes per side or until lightly browned.

4. Add sauce mixture to skillet with salt and black pepper to taste. Reduce heat to medium and simmer 12 to 15 minutes. Serve over noodles.

Makes 4 servings

Prep and Cook Time: 30 minutes

Chicken Cacciatore

Roasted Chicken Salad

2 cups cubed TYSON®
   Roasted Chicken
4 tablespoons mayonnaise
3 tablespoons sweet relish
1 tablespoon finely
   chopped celery
1 teaspoon finely chopped
   onion
¼ teaspoon mustard
⅛ teaspoon garlic salt
   Salt and black pepper to
   taste

PREP: CLEAN: Wash hands. In large bowl, combine all ingredients except chicken; mix well. Stir in chicken. Cover; chill thoroughly.

SERVE: Serve on a bed of lettuce leaves, in tomato cups or on kaiser rolls.

CHILL: Refrigerate leftovers immediately.

Makes 2 servings

Prep Time: 5 minutes
Cook Time: none

Magical Tip

To make a tomato cup, first cut the tomato in half or slice off just the top. Use a spoon to scoop out the seeds and pulp. Drain the hollowed-out shells by turning them upside down onto paper towels and allowing them to stand 15 minutes.

Roasted Chicken Salad

Chicken Tetrazzini

½ cup chopped onion

½ cup chopped celery

¼ cup (½ stick) butter or margarine

1 can (13¾ ounces) chicken broth

1 package (8 ounces) PHILADELPHIA® Cream Cheese, cubed

¾ cup KRAFT® 100% Grated Parmesan Cheese, divided

1 package (7 ounces) spaghetti, cooked, drained

1 jar (6 ounces) whole mushrooms, drained

1 cup chopped cooked chicken or turkey

COOK and stir onion and celery in butter in large skillet on medium heat until tender. Add broth, cream cheese and ½ cup of the Parmesan cheese; cook on low heat until cream cheese is melted, stirring occasionally.

ADD all remaining ingredients except remaining Parmesan cheese; mix lightly. Spoon into 12×8-inch baking dish; sprinkle with remaining ¼ cup Parmesan cheese.

BAKE at 350°F for 30 minutes.   *Makes 6 servings*

Prep Time: 20 minutes
Bake Time: 30 minutes

Magical Tip

Two whole chicken breasts (about 10 ounces each) yield about 2 cups chopped cooked chicken; one broiling/frying chicken (about 3 pounds) yields about 2½ cups chopped cooked chicken.

Chicken Piquante with Rice

2 tablespoons vegetable oil

4 boneless, skinless
chicken breast halves
(about 1 ½ pounds)

2 tablespoons all-purpose
flour

1 cup chopped celery

½ cup chopped onion

¼ cup chopped fresh
parsley

1 pound tomatoes, peeled,
seeded and cut into
½-inch cubes

¼ to ½ teaspoon ground
red pepper

1 can (15 ounces) tomato
sauce

2 cups hot cooked rice

Heat oil in large skillet over high heat until hot. Add chicken; cook until brown on both sides. Remove from skillet; set aside. Reduce heat to low; add flour to oil left in skillet. Stir about 15 minutes or until brown, being careful not to burn. Add celery, onion and parsley; cook and stir 3 to 5 minutes. Return chicken to skillet; add tomatoes, pepper and tomato sauce. Cover and simmer 25 to 30 minutes or until chicken is no longer pink in center. Serve over hot rice. Garnish as desired.

Makes 4 servings

Favorite recipe from **USA Rice Federation**

Magical Tip

One pound of tomatoes equals about 3 medium globe tomatoes, 8 plum tomatoes or 2 cups chopped tomatoes.

Roast Chicken with Peppers

1 cut-up chicken (3 to
   3 ½ pounds)

3 tablespoons olive oil,
   divided

1 ½ tablespoons chopped
   fresh rosemary *or*
   1 ½ teaspoons dried
   rosemary, crushed

1 tablespoon fresh lemon
   juice

1 ¼ teaspoons salt, divided

¾ teaspoon freshly ground
   black pepper, divided

3 bell peppers (preferably
   1 red, 1 yellow and
   1 green)

1 medium onion

1. Heat oven to 375°F. Rinse chicken in cold water; pat dry with paper towel. Place in shallow roasting pan.

2. Combine 2 tablespoons oil, rosemary and lemon juice in small bowl; brush over chicken. Sprinkle 1 teaspoon salt and ½ teaspoon black pepper over chicken. Roast 15 minutes.

3. Cut bell peppers lengthwise into ½-inch-thick strips. Slice onion into thin wedges. Toss vegetables with remaining 1 tablespoon oil, ¼ teaspoon salt and ¼ teaspoon black pepper in large bowl. Spoon vegetables around chicken; roast until vegetables are tender and chicken is cooked through, about 40 minutes. Serve chicken with vegetables and pan juices. Garnish as desired. *Makes 6 servings*

Magical Tip

There are several ways to test chicken to see if it is completely cooked. The most accurate method for whole chickens is to use a meat thermometer. Before roasting, insert the thermometer into the thickest part of the inner thigh away from any bones. Or, measure the temperature in the same location of the chicken with a handy, instant-read thermometer inserted just before the reading is taken and then removed. The chicken is done when the temperature registers 180°F.

Roast Chicken with Peppers

Chicken Pot Pie

All-Time Favorites

2 cups cut-up cooked chicken

1 package (10 ounces) frozen mixed vegetables, thawed

1¼ cups milk

1 envelope LIPTON® RECIPE SECRETS® Garlic Mushroom Soup Mix

1 pie crust or pastry for single-crust pie

1. Preheat oven to 400°F. In large bowl, combine chicken and vegetables; set aside.

2. In small saucepan, bring milk and soup mix to a boil over medium heat, stirring occasionally. Cook 1 minute. Stir into chicken mixture.

3. Pour into 9-inch pie plate. Top with pie crust. Press pastry around edge of pie plate to seal; trim excess pastry, then flute edges. With tip of knife, make small slits in pastry.

4. Bake uncovered 35 minutes or until crust is golden.

Makes 4 servings

Magical Tip

To make a pie crust, stir together 1 cup all-purpose flour and ¼ teaspoon salt in a large bowl. Cut in ⅓ cup vegetable shortening with a pastry blender or two knives until pieces are the size of small peas. Gradually add 3 to 4 tablespoons cold water, tossing mixture with a fork to incorporate just enough moisture for the mixture to be formed into a ball. Flatten the ball on a lightly floured board, and roll it out to an 11-inch circle.

Chicken Pot Pie

Southern Fried Chicken

2½ to 3 pounds frying
    chicken pieces
    WESSON® Vegetable Oil
2 cups self-rising flour
2 teaspoons salt
1 teaspoon pepper
1 teaspoon paprika
1 teaspoon onion powder
½ teaspoon ground sage
¼ teaspoon garlic powder
2 eggs beaten with
    2 tablespoons water

Rinse chicken and pat dry; set aside. Fill a large deep-fry pot or electric skillet to no more than half its depth with Wesson® Oil. Heat oil to 325°F to 350°F. In bag, combine flour and seasonings. Shake chicken, one piece at a time, in flour mixture until coated. Dip in egg mixture, then shake again in flour mixture until completely coated. Fry chicken, a few pieces at a time, skin side down, for 10 to 14 minutes. Turn and fry chicken 10 minutes, covered, then 3 to 5 minutes, uncovered, or until chicken is tender and juices run clear. Drain on paper towels. Let stand 7 minutes before serving.

Makes 4 to 6 servings

Magical Tip

Always use tongs to turn chicken pieces over during cooking. This prevents the skin from being pierced, keeping the natural juices sealed inside the skin.

Southern Fried Chicken

Coq au Vin

4 slices thick-cut bacon

2 cups frozen pearl onions, thawed

1 cup sliced button mushrooms

1 clove garlic, minced

1 teaspoon dried thyme leaves

⅛ teaspoon black pepper

6 boneless skinless chicken breast halves (about 2 pounds)

½ cup dry red wine

¾ cup reduced-sodium chicken broth

¼ cup tomato paste

3 tablespoons all-purpose flour

Hot cooked egg noodles (optional)

SLOW COOKER DIRECTIONS

Cook bacon in medium skillet over medium heat; drain and crumble. Layer ingredients in slow cooker in the following order: onions, bacon, mushrooms, garlic, thyme, pepper, chicken, wine and broth. Cover and cook on LOW 6 to 8 hours.

Remove chicken and vegetables; cover and keep warm. Ladle ½ cup cooking liquid into small bowl; allow to cool slightly. Turn slow cooker to HIGH; cover. Mix reserved liquid, tomato paste and flour until smooth. Return mixture to slow cooker; cover and cook 15 minutes or until thickened. Serve chicken, vegetables and sauce over hot noodles, if desired.

Makes 6 servings

Magical Tip

Coq au Vin is a classical French dish made with bone-in chicken, salt pork or bacon, brandy, red wine and herbs. The dish originated when farmers needed a way to cook old chickens that could no longer breed. A slow, moist cooking method was the perfect way to tenderize the tough old birds.

Coq au Vin

Chicken Gumbo

3 tablespoons vegetable oil

1 pound boneless skinless chicken breasts, cut into 1-inch pieces

½ pound smoked sausage,* cut into ¾-inch slices

1 bag (16 ounces) BIRDS EYE® frozen Farm Fresh Mixtures Broccoli, Corn and Red Peppers

1 can (14½ ounces) stewed tomatoes

1½ cups water

*For a spicy gumbo, use andouille sausage. Any type of kielbasa or turkey kielbasa can also be used.

• Heat oil in large saucepan over high heat. Add chicken and sausage; cook until browned, about 8 minutes.

• Add vegetables, tomatoes and water; bring to boil. Reduce heat to medium; cover and cook 5 to 6 minutes. Garnish as desired.   *Makes 4 to 6 servings*

Prep Time: 5 minutes
Cook Time: 20 minutes

Magical Tip

A Creole specialty that can most likely be traced to Africa, gumbo is a hearty, spicy stew that usually includes combinations of meat, sausage, poultry, seafood, tomatoes and vegetables. This New Orleans classic begins with a roux of flour and fat that has been allowed to brown over low heat to develop a rich flavor. The gumbo may also include okra or filé powder (obtained from sassafras root) for thickening.

Chicken Gumbo

Classic Arroz con Pollo

2 tablespoons olive oil

1 cut-up chicken

2 cups uncooked rice*

1 cup chopped onion

1 medium-size red bell pepper, chopped

1 medium-size green bell pepper, chopped

1 clove garlic, minced

1½ teaspoons salt, divided

1½ teaspoons dried basil leaves

4 cups chicken broth

1 tablespoon lime juice

⅛ teaspoon ground saffron or ½ teaspoon ground turmeric

1 bay leaf

2 cups chopped tomatoes

½ teaspoon black pepper

1 cup fresh or frozen green peas

Fresh basil for garnish

*Recipe based on regular-milled long grain white rice.

Heat oil in large Dutch oven over medium-high heat until hot. Add chicken; cook 10 minutes or until brown, turning occasionally. Remove chicken; keep warm. Add rice, onion, red bell pepper, green bell pepper, garlic, ¾ teaspoon salt and dried basil to pan; cook and stir 5 minutes or until vegetables are tender and rice is browned. Add broth, lime juice, saffron and bay leaf. Bring to a boil; stir in tomatoes. Arrange chicken on top and sprinkle with remaining ¾ teaspoon salt and black pepper. Cover; reduce heat to low. Cook 20 minutes more. Stir in peas; cover and cook 10 minutes more or until fork can be inserted into chicken with ease and juices run clear, not pink. Remove bay leaf. Garnish with fresh basil. Serve immediately. *Makes 8 servings*

Favorite recipe from **USA Rice Federation**

Chicken Stew with Dumplings

2 tablespoons vegetable oil

2 cups sliced carrots

1 cup chopped onion

1 large green bell pepper, sliced

½ cup sliced celery

2 cans (about 14 ounces each) fat-free reduced-sodium chicken broth, divided

¼ cup plus 2 tablespoons all-purpose flour

2 pounds boneless skinless chicken breasts, cut into 1-inch pieces

3 medium potatoes, unpeeled, cut into 1-inch pieces

6 ounces mushrooms, halved

¾ cup frozen peas

1 teaspoon dried basil leaves

¾ teaspoon dried rosemary leaves

¼ teaspoon dried tarragon leaves

¾ to 1 teaspoon salt

¼ teaspoon black pepper

HERB DUMPLINGS

2 cups biscuit mix

½ teaspoon dried basil leaves

½ teaspoon dried rosemary leaves

¼ teaspoon dried tarragon leaves

⅔ cup reduced-fat (2%) milk

1. Heat oil in 4-quart Dutch oven over medium heat until hot. Add carrots, onion, bell pepper and celery; cook and stir 5 minutes or until onion is tender. Stir in chicken broth, reserving ½ cup; bring to a boil.

2. Mix reserved ½ cup broth and flour in medium bowl; stir into boiling mixture. Boil, stirring constantly, 1 minute or until thickened.

3. Stir chicken, potatoes, mushrooms, peas and herbs into mixture. Reduce heat to low; simmer, covered, 18 to 20 minutes or until vegetables are almost tender and chicken is no longer pink in center. Add salt and black pepper.

4. For Herb Dumplings, combine biscuit mix and herbs in small bowl; stir in milk to form soft dough. Spoon dumpling mixture on top of stew in 8 large spoonfuls. Reduce heat to low. Cook, uncovered, 10 minutes. Cover and cook 10 minutes or until biscuits are tender and toothpick inserted in center comes out clean. Serve in shallow bowls. *Makes 8 servings*

Make-Ahead Time: up to 2 days before serving
Final Prep and Cook Time: about 1 hour

Chicken Stew with Dumplings

Chicken Vesuvio

All-Time Favorites

1 whole chicken (about
    3 ¾ pounds)
¼ cup olive oil
3 tablespoons lemon juice
4 cloves garlic, minced
3 large baking potatoes
  Salt
  Lemon pepper

Preheat oven to 375°F. Place chicken, breast side down, on rack in large shallow roasting pan. Combine olive oil, lemon juice and garlic in medium bowl; brush half of oil mixture over chicken. Set aside remaining oil mixture. Roast chicken, uncovered, 30 minutes.

Meanwhile, peel potatoes; cut lengthwise into quarters. Turn chicken, breast side up. Arrange potatoes around chicken in roasting pan. Brush chicken and potatoes with remaining oil mixture; sprinkle with salt and lemon pepper seasoning to taste. Roast chicken and potatoes, basting occasionally with pan juices, 50 minutes or until meat thermometer inserted into thickest part of chicken thigh, not touching bone, registers 180°F and potatoes are tender. Garnish as desired. *Makes 4 to 6 servings*

Chicken Vesuvio

Big Easy Chicken Creole

1 package (about
    2 ½ pounds) PERDUE®
    Fresh Split Skinless
    Chicken Breasts

1 ½ to 2 teaspoons Creole or
    Cajun seasoning

    Salt to taste

2 tablespoons canola oil

½ green bell pepper,
    seeded and chopped
    (about ¾ cup)

1 small onion, peeled and
    chopped (about
    ¾ cup)

1 can (14 ½ ounces) Cajun-
    or Mexican-style
    tomatoes

¼ cup white wine (optional)

2 tablespoons minced fresh
    parsley (optional)

    Hot cooked rice

With sharp knife, make 3 to 4 parallel slashes in each piece of chicken. Rub with seasoning mixture and salt, getting seasonings into slashes. In large skillet over medium heat, heat oil. Add chicken and cook 5 to 6 minutes per side, until browned. Remove and set aside. Add pepper and onion to skillet; sauté 2 to 3 minutes until softened. Stir in tomatoes and wine. Return chicken to pan. Partially cover with lid and reduce heat to medium-low. Simmer 30 to 35 minutes, until chicken is tender and cooked through (meat thermometer inserted in thickest part of breast should register 170°F). Sprinkle with parsley; serve over hot, fluffy rice.

Makes 4 servings

Magical Tip

To slice or chop a bell pepper, stand it on its end on a cutting board. Cut off 3 to 4 lengthwise slices from the sides with a utility knife, cutting close to, but not through, the stem. Discard the stem and seeds. Scrape out any remaining seeds and rinse the inside of the pepper under cold running water. Slice each piece lengthwise into long strips or cut into pieces.

Paella Valenciana

2 tablespoons vegetable oil

2 boneless, skinless chicken breasts halves (about ½ pound), cut into 1-inch strips

12 medium shrimp, peeled and deveined

½ cup chopped onion

2 medium red or green bell peppers, chopped

2 cups long-grain rice

2 cans (14½ ounces each) chicken broth

1 can (14½ ounces) whole peeled tomatoes, undrained, cut up

1 package (10 ounces) frozen peas, thawed

1 tablespoon LAWRY'S® Seasoned Salt

1 teaspoon LAWRY'S® Garlic Powder with Parsley

½ teaspoon hot pepper sauce

¼ cup sliced green olives

In paella pan or large skillet, heat oil. Add chicken and cook over medium-high heat until browned. Add shrimp and cook until pink; remove and set aside. Keep warm. In same skillet, cook onion and bell peppers. Add rice, broth and tomatoes; bring to a boil over medium-high heat. Reduce heat to low; cover and simmer 25 minutes. Add peas, Seasoned Salt, Garlic Powder with Parsley, hot pepper sauce and reserved chicken and shrimp mixture; mix well. Heat 10 minutes. Stir in olives.   *Makes 6 servings*

Hint: For a more Spanish-style dish, add finely chopped clams.

Magical Tip

Paella is a Spanish rice, vegetable and meat dish that originated in Valencia. Its name comes from the special wide and shallow two-handled pan in which it was traditionally prepared and served.

Chicken-Pesto Pizza

8 ounces chicken tenders
  Nonstick cooking spray
1 medium onion, thinly
  sliced
⅓ cup prepared pesto
3 medium plum tomatoes,
  thinly sliced
1 (14-inch) prepared pizza
  crust
1 cup (4 ounces) shredded
  mozzarella cheese

1. Preheat oven to 450°F. Cut chicken tenders into bite-size pieces. Coat medium nonstick skillet with cooking spray; cook and stir chicken over medium heat 2 minutes. Add onion and pesto; cook and stir about 3 minutes or until chicken is cooked through.

2. Arrange tomato slices and chicken mixture on pizza crust to within 1 inch of edge. Sprinkle cheese over topping. Bake 8 minutes or until pizza is hot and cheese is melted and bubbly.   *Makes 6 servings*

Prep and Cook Time: 22 minutes

Magical Tip

From the Italian word meaning *paste,* pesto is a green uncooked sauce from the Ligurian region of Italy made from fresh basil, garlic, pine nuts, Parmesan cheese and olive oil. The ingredients are mashed together, traditionally in a mortar with a pestle, but today, more likely in a food processor. While primarily served with pasta, pesto sauce is also added to minestrone soup, marinades and salad dressings.

Chicken-Pesto Pizza

Chicken Fried Rice

1 bag SUCCESS® Rice

½ pound boneless skinless chicken, cut into ½-inch pieces

½ teaspoon salt

¼ teaspoon pepper

2 tablespoons vegetable oil

1 clove garlic, minced

½ teaspoon grated fresh ginger

2 cups diagonally sliced green onions

1 cup sliced fresh mushrooms

2 tablespoons reduced-sodium soy sauce

1 teaspoon sherry

1 teaspoon Asian-style hot chili sesame oil (optional)

Prepare rice according to package directions.

Sprinkle chicken with salt and pepper; set aside. Heat oil in large skillet over medium-high heat. Add garlic and ginger; cook and stir 1 minute. Add chicken; stir-fry until no longer pink in center. Add green onions and mushrooms; stir-fry until tender. Stir in soy sauce, sherry and sesame oil. Add rice; heat thoroughly, stirring occasionally. *Makes 6 servings*

Magical Tip

For fresh grated ginger, first peel away the rough outer skin, then grate the flesh on a ginger grater (sold in many Asian markets) or other fine grater. For an even faster alternative, use a garlic press to mince a smal peeled chunk of ginger.

Chicken Fried Rice

Parmesan Chicken Breasts

½ cup KRAFT® 100% Grated Parmesan Cheese

¼ cup dry bread crumbs

1 teaspoon each dried oregano leaves and parsley flakes

¼ teaspoon each paprika, salt and black pepper

6 boneless skinless chicken breast halves (about 2 pounds)

2 tablespoons butter or margarine, melted

MIX cheese, crumbs and seasonings.

DIP chicken in butter; coat with cheese mixture. Place in 15×10×1-inch baking pan sprayed with no stick cooking spray.

BAKE at 400°F for 20 to 25 minutes or until cooked through.   *Makes 6 servings*

Spicy: Substitute ⅛ to ¼ teaspoon ground red pepper for black pepper.

Prep Time: 10 minutes
Bake Time: 25 minutes

Magical Tip

To make dry bread crumbs, bake cubed day-old dry bread on a baking sheet in a 325°F oven until very dry and lightly browned. Place them in a food processor or blender and process until fine crumbs are formed. Or, place toasted bread in a resealable plastic bag and seal. Roll with a rolling pin until fine crumbs are formed. To season dry bread crumbs, add dried herbs to the bread before processing.

Parmesan Chicken Breasts

The Speedy
Skillet

Chicken and Linguine in Creamy Tomato Sauce

1 tablespoon olive or
    vegetable oil
1 pound boneless, skinless
    chicken breasts, cut
    into ½-inch strips
1 jar (26 to 28 ounces)
    RAGÚ® Old World Style®
    Pasta Sauce
2 cups water
8 ounces linguine or
    spaghetti, uncooked
½ cup whipping or heavy
    cream
1 tablespoon fresh basil
    leaves, chopped, *or*
    ½ teaspoon dried
    basil leaves, crushed

1. In 12-inch skillet, heat oil over medium heat and brown chicken. Remove chicken and set aside.

2. In same skillet, stir in Ragú Pasta Sauce and water. Bring to a boil over high heat. Stir in uncooked linguine and return to a boil. Reduce heat to low and simmer covered, stirring occasionally, 15 minutes or until linguine is tender.

3. Stir in cream and basil. Return chicken to skillet and cook 5 minutes or until chicken is no longer pink.

Makes 4 servings

Prep Time: 10 minutes
Cook Time: 30 minutes

Chicken and Linguine in Creamy Tomato Sauce

Chicken Milano

2 cloves garlic, minced

4 boneless, skinless chicken breast halves (about 1¼ pounds)

½ teaspoon dried basil leaves, crushed

⅛ teaspoon crushed red pepper flakes (optional)

Salt and black pepper

1 tablespoon olive oil

1 can (14½ ounces) DEL MONTE® Diced Tomatoes with Basil, Garlic & Oregano, undrained

1 can (14½ ounces) DEL MONTE® Cut Green Italian Beans, drained

¼ cup whipping cream

1. Rub garlic over chicken. Sprinkle with basil and red pepper. Season with salt and black pepper.

2. Brown chicken in oil in skillet over medium-high heat. Stir in undrained tomatoes.

3. Cover; simmer 5 minutes. Uncover; reduce heat to medium and cook 8 to 10 minutes or until liquid is slightly thickened and chicken is tender.

4. Stir in green beans and cream; heat through. Do not boil.   *Makes 4 servings*

Prep and Cook Time: 25 minutes

20 Minute Chicken & Brown Rice Pilaf

1 tablespoon vegetable oil

4 boneless skinless chicken breast halves

1 can (10½ ounces) chicken broth

½ cup water

1 cup sliced fresh mushrooms

1 small onion, chopped

1 cup frozen peas

2 cups MINUTE® Brown Rice, uncooked

HEAT oil in skillet. Add chicken; cook until browned. Remove chicken.

ADD chicken broth and water; stir. Heat to a boil.

STIR in mushrooms, onion, peas and rice. Top with chicken; cover. Cook on low heat 5 minutes or until chicken is cooked through. Let stand 5 minutes.

Makes 4 servings

Chicken Milano

VELVEETA® 15 Minute
Cheesy Chicken & Vegetable Rice

1 tablespoon oil

4 small boneless skinless chicken breast halves (about 1 pound)

1 can (14½ ounces) chicken broth or 1¾ cups water

2 cups MINUTE® White Rice, uncooked

1 package (16 ounces) frozen vegetable blend (such as broccoli, cauliflower and carrots), thawed, drained

¾ pound (12 ounces) VELVEETA® Pasteurized Prepared Cheese Product, cut up

1. Heat oil in large nonstick skillet on medium-high heat. Add chicken; cover. Cook 4 minutes on each side or until cooked through. Remove chicken from skillet.

2. Add broth to skillet. Bring to boil.

3. Stir in rice, vegetables and Velveeta. Top with chicken; cover. Cook on low heat 5 minutes. Stir until Velveeta is melted.   *Makes 4 servings*

Note: Increase oil to 2 tablespoons if using regular skillet.

Chicken Fajitas

2 tablespoons olive or vegetable oil

2 medium red and/or green bell peppers, sliced

1 pound boneless, skinless chicken breasts, sliced

1 envelope LIPTON® RECIPE SECRETS® Onion Soup Mix

½ cup water

Flour tortillas, heated

1. In 12-inch nonstick skillet, heat oil over medium-high heat and cook red peppers 2 minutes. Add chicken and cook 4 minutes or until lightly browned.

2. Stir in soup mix blended with water. Simmer 2 minutes or until chicken is no longer pink. Serve in warm tortillas.   *Makes 4 servings*

Prep Time: 10 minutes
Cook Time: 8 minutes

VELVEETA® 15 Minute Cheesy Chicken & Vegetable Rice

Chicken Breasts Florentine

2 pounds boneless, skinless chicken breasts

¼ cup all-purpose flour

2 eggs, well beaten

⅔ cup seasoned dry bread crumbs

¼ cup BERTOLLI® Olive Oil

1 medium clove garlic, finely chopped

½ cup dry white wine

1 envelope LIPTON® RECIPE SECRETS® Golden Onion Soup Mix

1½ cups water

2 tablespoons finely chopped fresh parsley

⅛ teaspoon ground black pepper

Hot cooked rice pilaf or white rice

Hot cooked spinach

Dip chicken in flour, then eggs, then bread crumbs.

In 12-inch skillet, heat oil over medium heat and cook chicken until almost done. Remove chicken. Reserve 1 tablespoon drippings. Add garlic and wine to reserved drippings and cook over medium heat 5 minutes. Stir in soup mix thoroughly blended with water; bring to a boil. Return chicken to skillet and simmer covered 10 minutes or until chicken is no longer pink and sauce is slightly thickened. Stir in parsley and pepper. To serve, arrange chicken over hot rice and spinach; garnish as desired.

Makes about 6 servings

Magical Tip

"Florentine" refers to *à la florentine*, which is the phrase used to describe a French preparation method associated with the cuisine of Florence, Italy. Florentine dishes typically consist of the main ingredient served on a bed of spinach with a sauce over the top.

Chicken Broccoli Frittata

1 cup chopped fresh
    broccoli flowerettes

½ cup chopped cooked
    chicken

¼ cup chopped tomato

¼ cup chopped onion

¼ teaspoon dried tarragon
    leaves

1 tablespoon
    FLEISCHMANN'S®
    Original Margarine

1 cup EGG BEATERS®
    Healthy Real Egg
    Product

In 10-inch nonstick skillet, over medium heat, sauté broccoli, chicken, tomato, onion and tarragon in margarine until broccoli is tender-crisp. Reduce heat to low. Pour Egg Beaters evenly into skillet over chicken mixture. Cover; cook for 5 to 7 minutes or until cooked on bottom and almost set on top. Slide onto serving platter; cut into wedges to serve. *Makes 2 servings*

Prep Time: 15 minutes
Cook Time: 11 minutes

Mediterranean Chicken Skillet

1 tablespoon olive oil

1 package (about 1 pound)
    PERDUE® Fresh Italian
    Seasoned, Boneless
    Chicken Breasts

2 cups chopped fresh
    tomatoes or 1 can
    (14½ ounces) diced
    Italian stewed
    tomatoes

    Salt and ground pepper
    to taste

½ cup shredded Italian
    cheese blend or
    mozzarella

⅓ cup Italian olives

In large, nonstick skillet over medium heat, heat oil. Cook chicken 3 to 4 minutes per side, until browned. Add tomatoes and salt and pepper; reduce heat to medium-low. Cover and simmer 10 to 15 minutes, or until chicken is cooked through. To serve, top with cheese and olives. *Makes 4 servings*

Prep Time: 6 to 8 minutes
Cook Time: 20 to 25 minutes

Super Speedy Chicken on Angel Hair Pasta

1 package (12 ounces)
    angel hair pasta
3 boneless skinless chicken
    breast halves
    (12 ounces)
2 cups baby carrots
1 tablespoon olive oil
2 cups broccoli florets
¼ cup water
1 teaspoon instant chicken
    bouillon
1 jar (28 ounces) chunky-
    style pasta sauce
⅓ cup grated Parmesan
    cheese

1. Cook pasta according to package directions.

2. While pasta is cooking, cut chicken into 1-inch cubes. Cut carrots in half lengthwise.

3. Heat oil in large nonstick skillet over medium heat. Add chicken; cook and stir 5 minutes. Stir in carrots, broccoli, water and chicken bouillon. Reduce heat to low; cover and cook 5 minutes or until vegetables are crisp-tender.

4. Bring pasta sauce to a boil in medium saucepan over high heat. Place pasta on plates; top with hot pasta sauce and chicken and vegetable mixture. Sprinkle with cheese. *Makes 6 servings*

Prep and Cook Time: 25 minutes

Walnut Chicken Piccata

1 pound boneless, skinless
    chicken breasts
¼ cup all-purpose flour
2 tablespoons olive oil
½ cup chicken broth
½ cup white wine
¼ cup lemon juice
½ cup PLANTERS® Walnut
    Pieces, toasted and
    chopped
   Hot cooked rice or
    noodles
   Chopped parsley

1. Coat chicken with flour, shaking off excess.

2. Brown chicken breasts in olive oil in large skillet over medium-high heat for 3 minutes on each side. Add chicken broth, wine and lemon juice; heat to a boil. Reduce heat; simmer for 12 to 15 minutes or until chicken is cooked.

3. Add walnuts; heat through. Serve over rice or noodles; sprinkle with parsley. *Makes 4 servings*

Super Speedy Chicken on Angel Hair Pasta

Country French Chicken Skillet

2 tablespoons margarine or butter

1 ½ pounds boneless, skinless chicken breast halves

1 cup water

1 package KNORR® Recipe Classics™ Vegetable or Spring Vegetable Soup, Dip and Recipe Mix

¼ teaspoon dried dill weed (optional)

½ cup sour cream

• In large skillet, melt margarine over medium-high heat and brown chicken, turning occasionally, 5 minutes.

• Stir in water, recipe mix and dill weed. Bring to a boil over high heat. Reduce heat to low and simmer covered, stirring occasionally, 10 minutes or until chicken is no longer pink. Remove chicken to serving platter and keep warm.

• Remove skillet from heat; stir in sour cream. Spoon sauce over chicken and serve, if desired, with noodles.

Makes 4 to 6 servings

Prep Time: 5 minutes
Cook Time: 16 minutes

Chicken Sloppy Joes

1 tablespoon vegetable oil

1 pound ground chicken

1 green bell pepper, chopped

1 medium onion, chopped

2 cans (15 ounces each) sloppy joe sauce

3 cups cooked rice

6 hamburger buns

Heat oil in large skillet over medium-high heat until hot. Add chicken; cook and stir 4 to 6 minutes or until no longer pink. Stir in pepper and onion; cook 1 to 3 minutes. Add sloppy joe sauce. Cook over medium heat about 8 to 10 minutes, stirring occasionally. Stir in rice; cook until thoroughly heated. To serve, spoon into hamburger buns.

Makes 6 servings

Favorite recipe from USA Rice Federation

Country French Chicken Skillet

Cajun Chili

6 ounces spicy sausage
links, sliced

4 boneless, skinless
chicken thighs, cut into
cubes

1 medium onion, chopped

⅛ teaspoon cayenne
pepper

1 can (15 ounces) black-
eyed peas or kidney
beans, drained

1 can (14½ ounces) DEL
MONTE® Zesty Diced
Tomatoes with Mild
Green Chilies

1 medium green bell
pepper, chopped

1. Lightly brown sausage in large skillet over medium-high heat. Add chicken, onion and cayenne pepper; cook until browned. Drain.

2. Stir in remaining ingredients. Cook 5 minutes, stirring occasionally.   *Makes 4 servings*

Prep and Cook Time: 20 minutes

Broccoli Chicken au Gratin

1 (6.5-ounce) package
RICE-A-RONI® Broccoli
Au Gratin

2½ tablespoons margarine or
butter

¾ pound boneless, skinless
chicken breasts, cut
into thin strips

2 cups frozen chopped
broccoli

1 cup fresh sliced
mushrooms

¼ teaspoon coarse ground
black pepper

1. In large skillet over medium heat, sauté rice-pasta mix with margarine until pasta is light golden brown.

2. Slowly stir in 2¼ cups water, chicken and Special Seasonings; bring to a boil. Reduce heat to low. Cover; simmer 10 minutes.

3. Stir in broccoli, mushrooms and pepper. Cover; cook 5 to 10 minutes or until rice is tender and chicken is no longer pink inside. Let stand 3 to 5 minutes before serving.   *Makes 4 servings*

Prep Time: 5 minutes
Cook Time: 30 minutes

Cajun Chili

Skillet Chicken Cacciatore

2 tablespoons olive or
  vegetable oil
1 cup sliced red onion
1 medium green bell
  pepper, cut into strips
  (about 1 cup)
2 cloves garlic, minced
1 pound (about 4)
  boneless, skinless
  chicken breast halves
1 can (14.5 ounces)
  CONTADINA® Recipe
  Ready Diced Tomatoes
  with Italian Herbs,
  undrained
¼ cup dry white wine or
  chicken broth
½ teaspoon salt
¼ teaspoon ground black
  pepper
1 tablespoon chopped
  fresh basil *or*
  1 teaspoon dried basil
  leaves, crushed

1. Heat oil in large skillet over medium-high heat. Add onion, bell pepper and garlic; sauté 1 minute.

2. Add chicken; cook 6 to 8 minutes or until chicken is no longer pink in center.

3. Add undrained tomatoes, wine, salt and black pepper. Simmer, uncovered, 5 minutes. Serve over hot cooked rice or pasta, if desired. Sprinkle with basil. Garnish as desired. *Makes 6 servings*

Magical Tip

Cacciatore, Italian for "hunter," refers to dishes prepared "hunter's style." The most popular dish is Chicken Cacciatore. Recipes for this entrée usually include chicken cut into pieces, tomatoes or tomato sauce, mushrooms, onions, garlic and various herbs and spices. Chicken pieces are browned in a skillet, other ingredients are added, and the dish is simmered until the chicken is cooked. Cacciatore sometimes includes wine and may be served with pasta or rice.

Skillet Chicken Cacciatore

Cajun Stew

4 bacon slices

2 pounds chicken pieces

½ onion, sliced

1 package (1½ ounces) LAWRY'S® Original-Style Spaghetti Sauce Spices & Seasonings

1 can (14½ ounces) whole tomatoes, cut up

¼ to ½ cup water

1 package (10 ounces) frozen okra

1 package (10 ounces) frozen lima beans and corn

In large skillet or Dutch oven, fry bacon until slightly crisp; remove from pan and break into small pieces. Set aside. Brown chicken and onion in bacon drippings; drain fat. Add bacon, Spaghetti Sauce Spices & Seasonings, tomatoes and ¼ cup water; mix well. Bring to a boil over medium-high heat. Reduce heat to low; cover and simmer 30 minutes, stirring occasionally. Add vegetables and remaining ¼ cup water, if necessary. Cover and continue cooking 15 minutes. *Makes 6 servings*

Serving Suggestion: Serve in shallow soup bowls with lots of warmed, crusty French bread.

Hint: Use 1 package (1½ ounces) LAWRY'S® Extra Rich & Thick Spaghetti Sauce Seasoning Blend in place of 1 package (1½ ounces) LAWRY'S® Spaghetti Sauce Spices & Seasonings, if desired.

Sweet Spring Chicken

¼ cup light margarine (stick form)

1 package (about 1¼ pounds) PERDUE® Fresh Skinless Chicken Drumsticks

½ cup orange juice

2 tablespoons honey

2 teaspoons grated peeled fresh ginger

½ teaspoon ground cinnamon

In large nonstick skillet over medium-high heat, melt margarine. Add chicken; cook 6 to 8 minutes or until brown on all sides, turning often. In small bowl, combine orange juice, honey, ginger and cinnamon. Add mixture to skillet; reduce heat to medium-low. Cover and cook 25 to 35 minutes or until chicken is fork-tender, glazed and brown. Serve chicken with pan sauce. *Makes 3 to 4 servings*

Creamy Chicken Spaghetti

8 ounces spaghetti, uncooked

2 cups fresh or frozen chopped broccoli

4 boneless skinless chicken breast halves (about 1 ¼ pounds), cut into strips

¾ pound (12 ounces) VELVEETA® Pasteurized Prepared Cheese Product, cut up

1 can (10¾ ounces) condensed cream of mushroom soup

½ cup milk

1. Cook pasta as directed on package, adding broccoli during last 4 to 5 minutes of cooking time; drain. Return to same pan.

2. Spray skillet with no stick cooking spray. Add chicken; cook 4 to 5 minutes or until cooked through. Add Velveeta, soup and milk; stir on low heat until Velveeta is melted.

3. Add chicken mixture to pasta; toss to coat.

Makes 6 servings

Chicken and Pasta in Cream Sauce

5 ounces thin spaghetti, cooked, drained, kept warm

6 tablespoons unsalted butter

1 tablespoon Chef Paul Prudhomme's Poultry Magic®

½ pound diced boneless, skinless chicken breasts

¼ cup finely chopped green onions with tops

2 cups heavy cream or half-and-half

Melt butter in large skillet over medium heat. Add Poultry Magic® and chicken; cook 1 minute. Add onions; cook and stir 1 to 2 minutes. Gradually add cream, stirring until well blended. Bring to a boil. Reduce heat to low; simmer, uncovered, 2 to 3 minutes or until sauce starts to thicken, stirring frequently. Add pasta; toss and stir until pasta is heated through, about 2 minutes. Serve immediately.

Makes 2 main-dish servings

Skillet Chicken, Mushrooms and Vegetables

3 tablespoons bottled
Italian dressing,
divided
1 pound boneless skinless
chicken breasts
1 pound fresh white
mushrooms, sliced
2 plum tomatoes, diced
1 large carrot, cut into
matchsticks* or thinly
sliced
3 green onions, sliced
Steamed rice (optional)

*For carrot matchsticks, cut carrot into thin diagonal slices; stack 3 or 4 slices and cut into narrow sticks.

Heat 1 tablespoon dressing in large nonstick skillet over medium-high heat. Add chicken; cook about 2 minutes or until browned. Remove and set aside. Add remaining 2 tablespoons dressing to same skillet. Add mushrooms; cook 4 minutes, stirring frequently, until mushrooms begin to release their liquid. Stir in tomatoes, carrot and reserved chicken. Reduce heat; cover and simmer 10 minutes or until juices run clear when chicken is pierced with fork. Remove chicken and vegetables to heated platter. Cook sauce in skillet 2 minutes to thicken slightly; pour over chicken. Sprinkle with green onions. Serve with steamed rice, if desired.

Makes 4 servings

Preparation and Cooking Time: about 25 minutes

*Favorite recipe from **Mushroom Council***

15 Minute Chicken Parmesan Risotto

1 tablespoon vegetable oil
1 pound boneless skinless
chicken breasts, cut
into small pieces
1 large tomato (optional)
1 can (10¾ ounces) cream
of chicken soup
1⅔ cups milk
½ cup (2 ounces) KRAFT®
100% Grated
Parmesan Cheese
½ teaspoon Italian
seasoning (optional)
2 cups MINUTE® White Rice,
uncooked

HEAT oil in skillet. Add chicken; cook until lightly browned. While chicken is cooking, chop tomato.

ADD soup, milk, Parmesan cheese and seasoning; stir. Heat to a boil.

STIR in rice and tomato; cover. Cook on low heat 5 minutes or until cooked through. Stir.

Makes 4 servings

Note: Substitute any cream soup for cream of chicken soup.

Skillet Chicken, Mushrooms and Vegetables

Chicken Rosemary

2 boneless skinless chicken breast halves

1 teaspoon margarine

1 teaspoon olive oil
 Salt and pepper

½ small onion, sliced

1 large clove garlic, minced

½ teaspoon dried rosemary

⅛ teaspoon ground cinnamon

½ cup DOLE® Pineapple Juice

1 tablespoon orange marmalade

2 cups sliced DOLE® Carrots

Place chicken between 2 pieces of waxed paper or plastic wrap. Pound with flat side of meat mallet or rolling pin to ½-inch thickness. In medium skillet, brown chicken on both sides in margarine and oil. Sprinkle with salt and pepper. Stir in onion, garlic, rosemary and cinnamon. Cook and stir until onion is soft. Blend in juice and marmalade. Spoon over chicken. Cover; simmer 10 minutes. Stir in carrots. Cover; simmer 5 minutes or until carrots are tender-crisp and chicken is no longer pink in center. Garnish as desired.   *Makes 2 servings*

Prep Time: 10 minutes
Cook Time: 20 minutes

Busy Night Chicken Lo Mein

2 tablespoons margarine or butter

8 ounces boneless, skinless chicken breasts, cut into ½-inch pieces

¼ cup chopped green onions

1 (16-ounce) package frozen Oriental-style mixed vegetables

1 (4.8-ounce) package PASTA RONI® Angel Hair Pasta with Herbs

3 tablespoons teriyaki sauce

1. In large skillet over medium-high heat, melt margarine. Add chicken and onions; sauté 5 minutes or until chicken is no longer pink.

2. Stir in 2 cups water and vegetables; bring to a boil.

3. Stir in pasta and Special Seasonings. Reduce heat to medium. Gently boil uncovered 4 to 5 minutes or until pasta is tender, stirring frequently.

4. Stir in teriyaki sauce. Let stand 3 minutes before serving.   *Makes 4 servings*

Prep Time: 5 minutes
Cook Time: 15 minutes

Chicken Rosemary

Chicken Enchilada Skillet Casserole

The Speedy Skillet

1 bag (16 ounces) BIRDS EYE® frozen Farm Fresh Mixtures Broccoli, Corn & Red Peppers

1 package (1¼ ounces) taco seasoning mix

1 can (16 ounces) diced tomatoes, undrained

3 cups shredded cooked chicken

1 cup shredded Monterey Jack cheese

8 ounces tortilla chips

• In large skillet, combine vegetables, seasoning mix, tomatoes and chicken; bring to a boil over medium-high heat.

• Cover; cook 4 minutes or until vegetables are cooked and mixture is heated through.

• Sprinkle with cheese; cover and cook 2 minutes more or until cheese is melted.

• Serve with chips.   *Makes 4 servings*

Prep Time: 5 minutes
Cook Time: 10 minutes

Jiffy Chicken & Rice Gumbo

1 (6.9-ounce) package RICE-A-RONI® Chicken Flavor

1 small green bell pepper, coarsely chopped

2 tablespoons margarine or butter

1 pound boneless, skinless chicken breasts, cut into 1-inch pieces

1 (14½-ounce) can diced tomatoes with garlic and onion, undrained

¾ to 1 teaspoon Creole or Cajun seasoning*

*mixture of ½ teaspoon cayenne pepper, ¼ teaspoon dried oregano and ¼ teaspoon dried thyme may be substituted.

1. In large skillet over medium heat, sauté rice-vermicelli mix and bell pepper with margarine until vermicelli is golden brown.

2. Slowly stir in 2¼ cups water, chicken, tomatoes, Creole seasoning and Special Seasonings; bring to a boil. Reduce heat to low. Cover; simmer 15 to 20 minutes or until rice is tender.   *Makes 4 servings*

Prep Time: 5 minutes
Cook Time: 30 minutes

Chicken Enchilada Skillet Casserole

5-Ingredient Magic

Southern BBQ Chicken and Rice

1 cup UNCLE BEN'S®
  ORIGINAL CONVERTED®
  Brand Rice
4 TYSON® Individually
  Fresh Frozen® Chicken
  Half Breasts
1½ cups water
1 cup barbecue sauce,
  divided
1 package (6 half ears)
  frozen corn on the cob

COOK: CLEAN: Wash hands. In large skillet, combine water, rice, ¾ cup barbecue sauce and chicken. Bring to a boil. Cover. Reduce heat; simmer 25 minutes. Add corn; cook 15 to 20 minutes or until internal juices of chicken run clear. (Or insert instant-read meat thermometer in thickest part of chicken. Temperature should read 170°F.) Spoon remaining ¼ cup barbecue sauce over chicken. Remove from heat; let stand 5 minutes or until liquid is absorbed.

SERVE: Serve with extra barbecue sauce and corn bread, if desired.

CHILL: Refrigerate leftovers immediately.

Makes 4 servings

Prep Time: none
Cook Time: 40 to 45 minutes

Southern BBQ Chicken and Rice

Ranch Crispy Chicken

- ¼ cup unseasoned dry bread crumbs or cornflake crumbs
- 1 packet (1 ounce) HIDDEN VALLEY® Original Ranch® Salad Dressing & Recipe Mix
- 6 bone-in chicken pieces

Combine bread crumbs and salad dressing & recipe mix in a gallon-size Glad® Zipper Storage Bag. Add chicken pieces; seal bag. Shake to coat chicken. Bake chicken on ungreased baking pan at 375°F. for 50 minutes or until no longer pink in center and juices run clear.

Makes 4 to 6 servings

Garlic Herb Chicken and Rice Skillet

- 4 TYSON® Individually Fresh Frozen® Boneless, Skinless Chicken Breasts
- 1 box UNCLE BEN'S® COUNTRY INN® Chicken Flavored Rice
- 1¾ cups water
- 2 cups frozen broccoli, carrots and cauliflower mixture
- ¼ cup garlic and herb soft spreadable cheese

COOK: CLEAN: Wash hands. In large skillet, combine chicken, water and contents of seasoning packet. Bring to a boil. Cover. Reduce heat; simmer 10 minutes. Add rice, vegetables and cheese. Cook, covered, 10 to 15 minutes or until internal juices of chicken run clear. (Or insert instant-read meat thermometer in thickest part of chicken. Temperature should read 170°F.) Remove from heat; let stand 5 minutes or until liquid is absorbed.

SERVE: Dish out chicken onto individual plates and serve while hot.

CHILL: Refrigerate leftovers immediately.

Makes 4 servings

Prep Time: none
Cook Time: 25 to 30 minutes

Ranch Crispy Chicken

Country Chicken and Biscuits

1 can (10¾ ounces) condensed cream of celery soup

⅓ cup milk or water

4 boneless skinless chicken breast halves, cooked and cut into bite-sized pieces

1 can (14½ ounces) DEL MONTE® Cut Green Beans, drained

1 can (11 ounces) refrigerated biscuits

1. Preheat oven to 375°F.

2. Combine soup and milk in large bowl. Gently stir in chicken and green beans; season with pepper, if desired. Spoon into 11×7-inch microwavable dish.

3. Cover with plastic wrap; slit to vent. Microwave on HIGH 8 to 10 minutes or until heated through, rotating dish once. If using conventional oven, cover with foil and bake at 375°F, 20 to 25 minutes or until hot.

4. Separate biscuit dough into individual biscuits. Immediately arrange biscuits over hot mixture. Bake in conventional oven about 15 minutes or until biscuits are golden brown and baked through.

Makes 4 servings

Golden Chicken Nuggets

1 envelope LIPTON® RECIPE SECRETS® Golden Onion Soup Mix

½ cup plain dry bread crumbs

1½ pounds boneless, skinless chicken breasts, cut into 2-inch pieces

2 tablespoons margarine or butter, melted

1. Preheat oven to 425°F. In small bowl, combine soup mix and bread crumbs. Dip chicken in bread crumb mixture until evenly coated.

2. On lightly greased cookie sheet, arrange chicken; drizzle with margarine.

3. Bake uncovered 15 minutes or until chicken is no longer pink, turning once. *Makes 6 servings*

Tip: Also terrific with Lipton® Recipe Secrets® Onion Soup Mix, Onion Mushroom Soup Mix, or Savory Herb with Garlic Soup Mix.

Prep Time: 10 minutes
Cook Time: 15 minutes

Country Chicken and Biscuits

Garlic Mushroom Chicken Melt

4 boneless, skinless chicken breast halves (about 1 ¼ pounds)

1 envelope LIPTON® RECIPE SECRETS® Savory Herb with Garlic Soup Mix

1 can (14 ounces) diced tomatoes, undrained, or 1 large tomato, chopped

1 tablespoon olive or vegetable oil

½ cup shredded mozzarella or Monterey Jack cheese (about 2 ounces)

1. Preheat oven to 375°F. In 13×9-inch baking or roasting pan, arrange chicken. Pour soup mix blended with tomatoes and oil over chicken.

2. Bake uncovered 25 minutes or until chicken is no longer pink.

3. Sprinkle with mozzarella cheese and bake an additional 2 minutes or until cheese is melted.

Makes 4 servings

Minute® Easy Chicken Stir-Fry

3 cups sliced vegetables for stir fry (peppers, mushrooms, broccoli, carrots)

1 tablespoon oil

1 package (6 ounces) LOUIS RICH® Grilled *or* Teriyaki Chicken Breast Strips

½ cup bottled stir-fry *or* sweet 'n sour sauce

Hot cooked MINUTE® White Rice

COOK and stir vegetables in oil in medium skillet on medium-high heat 5 minutes or until tender-crisp.

ADD chicken breast strips and sauce; cover. Cook 2 minutes or until heated through.

SPOON over rice. *Makes 2 to 3 servings*

Prep Time: 10 minutes
Cook Time: 7 minutes

Garlic Mushroom Chicken Melt

Mile-High Enchilada Pie

8 (6-inch) corn tortillas

1 jar (12 ounces) prepared salsa

1 can (15½ ounces) kidney beans, rinsed and drained

1 cup shredded cooked chicken

1 cup shredded Monterey Jack cheese with jalapeño peppers

SLOW COOKER DIRECTIONS
Prepare foil handles for slow cooker (see below); place in slow cooker. Place 1 tortilla on bottom of slow cooker. Top with small amount of salsa, beans, chicken and cheese. Continue layering using remaining ingredients, ending with cheese. Cover and cook on LOW 6 to 8 hours or on HIGH 3 to 4 hours. Pull out by foil handles. Garnish as desired.

Makes 4 to 6 servings

Foil Handles: Tear off three 18×2-inch strips of heavy foil or use regular foil folded to double thickness. Crisscross foil strips in spoke design and place in slow cooker to make lifting of tortilla stack easier.

VELVEETA® Cheesy Italian Chicken

4 boneless skinless chicken breast halves (about 1¼ pounds)

1 can (15 ounces) chunky Italian-style tomato sauce or 1 jar (15 ounces) chunky spaghetti sauce

½ pound (8 ounces) VELVEETA® Pasteurized Prepared Cheese Product, cut up

Hot cooked pasta

1. Spray large skillet with no stick cooking spray. Add chicken; brown on medium-high heat 1 to 2 minutes on each side. Reduce heat to low.

2. Stir in tomato sauce; cover. Simmer 12 to 15 minutes or until chicken is cooked through.

3. Add Velveeta; cover. Cook on low heat until Velveeta is melted. Serve over pasta. *Makes 4 servings*

Prep Time: 5 minutes
Cook Time: 20 minutes

Mile-High Enchilada Pie

Basic Fried Chicken

5-Ingredient Magic

½ cup all-purpose flour
1 tablespoon seasoned salt
½ teaspoon ground black pepper
1 cut up chicken
Vegetable oil for frying

Combine flour, salt and pepper in gallon size plastic resealable food bag. Rinse chicken under cold running water; do not dry. Drop chicken, 2 to 3 pieces at a time, into flour mixture; shake to coat well. Heat ½ inch oil in large skillet over medium-high heat until hot. Place chicken, skin side down, in skillet. Turn pieces to brown evenly on all sides. Reduce heat to medium-low; cover and cook about 30 minutes or until fork can be inserted into chicken with ease and juices run clear, not pink. Drain on paper towels. Serve hot or cold.

Makes 4 servings

Variations: Add 1 teaspoon dry mustard and 1 teaspoon dried thyme or 1 teaspoon curry powder *or* ½ teaspoon lemon pepper and ½ teaspoon dried thyme to flour mixture. Continue as directed.

Favorite recipe from **National Chicken Council**

Herbed Chicken and Potatoes

2 medium all-purpose potatoes, thinly sliced (about 1 pound)
4 bone-in chicken breast halves (about 2 pounds)*
1 envelope LIPTON® RECIPE SECRETS® Savory Herb with Garlic Soup Mix
⅓ cup water
1 tablespoon olive or vegetable oil

*Substitution: Use 1 (2½- to 3-pound) chicken, cut into serving pieces.

1. Preheat oven to 425°F. In 13×9-inch baking or roasting pan, add potatoes; arrange chicken over potatoes.

2. Pour soup mix blended with water and oil over chicken and potatoes.

3. Bake uncovered 40 minutes or until chicken is no longer pink and potatoes are tender.

Makes 4 servings

Ranch Chicken with Cheese

½ cup HIDDEN VALLEY®
   Original Ranch®
   Dressing

1 tablespoon all-purpose
   flour

4 boneless, skinless
   chicken breast halves
   (about 1 pound)

¼ cup (1 ounce) shredded
   sharp Cheddar cheese

¼ cup grated Parmesan
   cheese

Combine dressing and flour in a shallow bowl. Coat each chicken breast with dressing mixture. Place on ungreased baking pan. Combine Cheddar and Parmesan cheeses; sprinkle on chicken. Bake at 375°F. for 25 minutes or until chicken is no longer pink in center and juices run clear.   *Makes 4 servings*

Chicken Tortellini Soup

1 can (49½ ounces)
   chicken broth

1 package PERDUE® SHORT
   CUTS® Fresh Italian
   Carved Chicken Breast

1 package (9 ounces) fresh
   pesto or cheese
   tortellini or tortelloni

1 cup fresh spinach or
   arugula leaves,
   shredded

¼ to ½ cup grated
   Parmesan cheese

In large saucepan over medium-high heat, bring broth to a boil. Add chicken and tortellini; cook 6 to 8 minutes, until pasta is tender, reducing heat to keep a gentle boil. Just before serving, stir in fresh spinach. Ladle soup into bowls and sprinkle with Parmesan cheese.   *Makes 4 servings*

Prep Time: 5 minutes
Cook Time: 15 minutes

VELVEETA® Cheesy Chicken Ranch Sandwiches

6 boneless skinless chicken breast halves (about 2 pounds)

⅔ cup KRAFT® Ranch Dressing, divided

½ pound (8 ounces) VELVEETA® Pasteurized Prepared Cheese Product, sliced

6 French bread rolls, split

Lettuce

1. Brush chicken with ⅓ cup of the dressing. Spray rack of broiler pan with no stick cooking spray. Place chicken on rack of broiler pan.

2. Broil 3 to 4 inches from heat 5 to 6 minutes on each side or until cooked through. Top chicken with Velveeta. Broil an additional 2 minutes or until Velveeta is melted.

3. Spread rolls with remaining dressing; fill with lettuce and chicken. *Makes 6 sandwiches*

Use Your Grill: Prepare chicken as directed. Grill over hot coals 5 to 6 minutes on each side or until cooked through. Top with Velveeta and continue grilling until Velveeta is melted. Continue as directed.

Prep Time: 5 minutes
Broil Time: 14 minutes

Chicken Nachos

22 (about 1 ounce) GUILTLESS GOURMET® Baked Tortilla Chips (yellow, red or blue corn)

½ cup (4 ounces) cooked and shredded boneless chicken breast

¼ cup chopped green onions

¼ cup (1 ounce) grated Cheddar cheese

Sliced green and red chilies (optional)

MICROWAVE DIRECTIONS

Spread tortilla chips on flat microwave-safe plate. Sprinkle chicken, onions and cheese over chips. Microwave on HIGH 30 seconds until cheese starts to bubble. Serve hot. Garnish with chilies, if desired.

Makes 22 nachos

Conventional Directions: Preheat oven to 325°F. Spread tortilla chips on baking sheet. Sprinkle chicken, onions and cheese over chips. Bake about 5 minutes or until cheese starts to bubble. Serve hot.

VELVEETA® Cheesy Chicken Ranch Sandwich

Roasted Chicken au Jus

1 envelope LIPTON® RECIPE
   SECRETS® Garlic
   Mushroom Soup Mix*
2 tablespoons olive or
   vegetable oil
1 (2½- to 3-pound)
   chicken, cut into
   serving pieces
½ cup hot water

*Also terrific with LIPTON® RECIPE
SECRETS® Savory Herb with Garlic
Soup Mix.

1. Preheat oven to 425°F. In large bowl, combine soup mix and oil; add chicken and toss until evenly coated.

2. In bottom of broiler pan without rack, arrange chicken. Roast chicken, basting occasionally, 40 minutes or until chicken is no longer pink.

3. Remove chicken to serving platter. Add hot water to pan and stir, scraping brown bits from bottom of pan. Serve sauce over chicken.   *Makes 4 servings*

Fantastic Feta Chicken

6 boneless skinless chicken
   breast halves (about
   2 pounds)
2 tablespoons lemon juice,
   divided
2 teaspoons chopped fresh
   oregano *or* ¼ teaspoon
   dried oregano leaves,
   crushed
¼ teaspoon fresh ground
   pepper
1 package (4 ounces)
   ATHENOS® Crumbled
   Feta Cheese

• Arrange chicken in 13×9-inch baking dish.

• Drizzle with 1 tablespoon of the juice. Sprinkle with oregano and pepper. Top with cheese; drizzle with remaining 1 tablespoon juice.

• Bake at 350°F for 30 to 35 minutes or until cooked through.   *Makes 6 servings*

Prep Time: 10 minutes
Bake Time: 35 minutes

Roasted Chicken au Jus

Garden Ranch Linguine with Chicken

8 ounces linguine, cooked & drained

2 cups cooked mixed vegetables, such as broccoli, cauliflower and bell peppers

2 cups cubed cooked chicken

1 cup prepared HIDDEN VALLEY® The Original Ranch® Salad Dressing

1 tablespoon grated Parmesan cheese

Combine all ingredients except cheese in a large saucepan; toss well. Heat through; sprinkle with cheese before serving.

Makes 4 servings

One-Dish Chicken Bake

1 package (6 ounces) STOVE TOP® Stuffing Mix for Chicken

4 boneless skinless chicken breast halves (about 1¼ pounds)

1 can (10¾ ounces) condensed cream of mushroom soup

⅓ cup BREAKSTONE® or KNUDSEN® Sour Cream or milk

1. STIR stuffing crumbs, contents of vegetable/seasoning packet, 1½ cups hot water and ¼ cup margarine, cut-up, just until moistened; set aside.

2. PLACE chicken in 12×8-inch baking dish. Mix soup and sour cream; pour over chicken. Top with stuffing.

3. BAKE at 375°F for 35 minutes or until chicken is cooked through.

Makes 4 servings

Prep Time: 10 minutes
Bake Time: 35 minutes

Garden Ranch Linguine with Chicken

Easy Chicken and Potato Dinner

1 package (2 pounds)
    bone-in chicken
    breasts or thighs
1 pound potatoes, cut into
    wedges
½ cup KRAFT® Zesty Italian
    Dressing
1 tablespoon Italian
    seasoning
½ cup KRAFT® 100%
    Grated Parmesan
    Cheese

• **PLACE** chicken and potatoes in 13×9-inch baking pan.

• **POUR** dressing over chicken and potatoes. Sprinkle evenly with Italian seasoning and cheese.

• **BAKE** at 400°F for 1 hour or until chicken is cooked through.   *Makes 4 servings*

Quick Chicken and Ravioli Marinara

1 tablespoon olive oil
1 yellow *or* green pepper,
    cut into strips
1 package (6 ounces)
    LOUIS RICH® Italian
    Style *or* Grilled Chicken
    Breast Strips
1 package (15 ounces)
    DI GIORNO® Marinara
    Sauce
1 package (9 ounces)
    DI GIORNO® Four
    Cheese Ravioli,
    cooked, drained

HEAT oil in skillet on medium-high heat. Add peppers; cook and stir 2 minutes.

STIR in chicken strips and sauce. Cook on medium heat 3 to 5 minutes or until thoroughly heated.

SERVE over hot ravioli. Top with DI GIORNO® Shredded Parmesan Cheese, if desired.

Makes 3 to 4 servings

Prep Time: 10 minutes
Cook Time: 10 minutes

Easy Chicken and Potato Dinner

4 boneless skinless chicken breast halves (about 1 ¼ pounds), cut into chunks

1 can (14½ ounces) chicken broth

2 cups (8 ounces) elbow macaroni, uncooked

¾ pound (12 ounces) VELVEETA® Pasteurized Prepared Cheese Product, cut up

1 package (10 ounces) frozen chopped broccoli, thawed

1. Spray large skillet with no stick cooking spray. Add chicken; cook and stir on medium-high heat 2 minutes or until no longer pink.

2. Stir in broth. Bring to boil. Stir in macaroni. Reduce heat to medium-low; cover. Simmer 8 to 10 minutes or until macaroni is tender.

3. Add Velveeta and broccoli; stir until Velveeta is melted.   *Makes 4 to 6 servings*

Cheesy Chicken & Broccoli Rice: Substitute 2 cups uncooked MINUTE® Rice for macaroni. Cook chicken as directed. Add broth; bring to boil. Add rice, Velveeta and broccoli; stir. Cover. Remove from heat. Let stand 10 minutes. Stir until melted.

Prep Time: 10 minutes
Cook Time: 15 minutes

VELVEETA® Cheesy Chicken & Broccoli Macaroni

Chicken Cacciatore Melt

4 TYSON® Fresh Boneless, Skinless Chicken Thigh Cutlets

2 tablespoons garlic oil

1 jar (28 ounces) spaghetti sauce

1 cup shredded mozzarella cheese

4 large slices crusty Italian bread, lightly toasted

COOK: CLEAN: Wash hands. In large skillet, heat oil. Add chicken and cook 3 minutes per side or until browned. Stir in spaghetti sauce. Cover and cook over medium heat 20 minutes or until internal juices of chicken run clear. (Or insert instant-read meat thermometer in thickest part of chicken. Temperature should read 180°F.) Divide cheese evenly over chicken. Cover and cook over medium heat 1 minute or until cheese is melted slightly.

SERVE: Serve over toasted Italian bread slices.

CHILL: Refrigerate leftovers immediately.

Makes 4 servings

Tip: Use mixture of 1 clove garlic, minced, and 2 tablespoons olive oil if garlic oil is not available. Fresh sliced mushrooms may be added to spaghetti sauce before heating, if desired.

Chicken Pizzawiches

1 package (12 ounces) frozen breaded chicken breast patties

1 cup shredded mozzarella cheese

1 jar (14 ounces) spaghetti sauce

½ cup HOLLAND HOUSE® Red Cooking Wine

4 sandwich buns

MICROWAVE DIRECTIONS

Microwave chicken patties as directed on package. Top each piece of chicken with ¼ cup mozzarella. Microwave at HIGH an additional 30 to 60 seconds. Place spaghetti sauce and cooking wine in microwavable bowl covered with waxed paper; microwave at HIGH 4 to 5 minutes, stirring once. Place chicken patties on buns; spoon sauce over patties. *Makes 4 servings*

Chicken Cacciatore Melt

Chicken & Creamy Garlic Sauce

1 teaspoon BERTOLLI®
    Olive Oil

4 boneless, skinless
    chicken breast halves

1 jar (16 ounces) RAGÚ®
    Cheese Creations!®
    Roasted Garlic
    Parmesan Sauce

1 small tomato, chopped

8 ounces rotelle pasta,
    cooked and drained

In 12-inch nonstick skillet, heat oil over medium heat and lightly brown chicken. Stir in Ragú Cheese Creations! Sauce and tomato. Simmer covered, stirring occasionally, 10 minutes or until chicken is no longer pink. To serve, spoon chicken and sauce over hot pasta. Garnish, if desired, with crisp-cooked crumbled bacon and chopped fresh basil.   *Makes 4 servings*

Chile Rellenos-Style Chicken

6 boneless skinless chicken
    breast halves

1 envelope SHAKE 'N
    BAKE® Seasoning and
    Coating Mixture—Hot
    & Spicy Recipe for
    Chicken

½ cup (2 ounces) shredded
    Cheddar or Monterey
    Jack cheese*

1 can (4 ounces) chopped
    green chilies, drained

    Salsa (optional)

*Or, use ¼ cup of each cheese.

HEAT oven to 400°F.

COAT chicken with coating mixture as directed on package.

BAKE 20 minutes on ungreased or foil-lined 15×10-inch metal baking pan. Mix cheese and chilies. Spoon over chicken. Bake 5 minutes or until chicken is cooked through and cheese is melted. Serve with salsa.
          Makes 4 servings

Prep Time: 5 minutes
Cook Time: 25 minutes

Chicken & Creamy Garlic Sauce

Cajun Chicken Bayou

2 cups water

1 can (10 ounces) diced
   tomatoes and green
   chilies, undrained

1 box UNCLE BEN'S®
   CHEF'S RECIPE™
   Traditional Red Beans
   & Rice

2 boneless, skinless
   chicken breasts (about
   8 ounces)

1. In large skillet, combine water, tomatoes, beans & rice and contents of seasoning packet; mix well.

2. Add chicken. Bring to a boil. Cover; reduce heat and simmer 20 minutes or until chicken is no longer pink in center.

Makes 2 servings

Hint: If you prefer a spicier dish, add hot pepper sauce just before serving.

Sweet 'n Spicy Chicken

1 bottle (8 ounces) WISH-
   BONE® Russian
   Dressing

1 envelope LIPTON® RECIPE
   SECRETS® Onion Soup
   Mix

1 jar (12 ounces) apricot
   preserves

2½- to 3-pound chicken, cut
   into serving pieces

Preheat oven to 425°F. In small bowl, combine Russian dressing, onion soup mix and preserves.

In 13×9-inch baking dish, arrange chicken; pour on dressing mixture. Bake uncovered, basting occasionally with dressing mixture, 40 minutes or until chicken is no longer pink. Serve, if desired, with hot cooked rice.

Makes about 6 servings

Cajun Chicken Bayou

Crispy Oven-Baked Chicken

4 boneless skinless chicken
   breast halves (about
   4 ounces each)

¾ cup GUILTLESS
   GOURMET® Roasted
   Red Pepper Salsa

Nonstick cooking spray

1 cup (3.5 ounces) crushed
   GUILTLESS GOURMET®
   Baked Tortilla Chips
   (yellow corn, red corn
   or chili lime)*

Cherry tomatoes and
   pineapple sage leaves
   (optional)

*Crush tortilla chips in the orginal bag
or between two pieces of waxed paper
with a rolling pin.

Wash chicken; pat dry with paper towels. Place chicken in shallow nonmetal pan or place in large resealable plastic food storage bag. Pour salsa over chicken. Cover with foil or seal bag; marinate in refrigerator 8 hours or overnight.

Preheat oven to 350°F. Coat baking sheet with cooking spray. Place crushed chips on waxed paper. Remove chicken from salsa, discarding salsa; roll chicken in crushed chips. Place on prepared baking sheet; bake 45 minutes or until chicken is no longer pink in center and chips are crisp. Serve hot. Garnish with tomatoes and sage, if desired. *Makes 4 servings*

Herb Batter Baked Chicken

⅔ cup prepared HIDDEN
   VALLEY® The Original
   Ranch® Salad Dressing

1 egg, lightly beaten

1 broiler-fryer chicken
   (about 3 pounds),
   cut up

½ cup all-purpose flour

2 cups cornflake crumbs

Preheat oven to 350°F. On shallow plate, combine salad dressing and egg; set aside. Rinse chicken; pat dry with paper towels. Roll chicken pieces in flour; dip into dressing mixture. Roll in cornflake crumbs. Place chicken on large foil-lined baking pan. Bake until tender, 45 to 50 minutes. *Makes 4 servings*

Crispy Oven-Baked Chicken

Hot off the
Grill

Grilled Lemon Chicken Dijon

⅓ cup HOLLAND HOUSE®
    White with Lemon
    Cooking Wine

⅓ cup olive oil

2 tablespoons Dijon
    mustard

1 teaspoon dried thyme
    leaves

2 whole chicken breasts,
    skinned, boned and
    halved

In shallow baking dish combine cooking wine, oil, mustard and thyme. Add chicken and turn to coat. Cover; marinate in refrigerator for 1 to 2 hours.

Prepare grill for direct cooking. Drain chicken, reserving marinade. Grill chicken over medium coals 15 to 20 minutes or until cooked through, turning once and basting with marinade.*   *Makes 4 servings*

*Do not baste during last 5 minutes of grilling.

Grilled Lemon Chicken Dijon

Rotisserie Chicken with Pesto Brush

2 BUTTERBALL® Fresh
   Young Roasters
¼ cup chopped fresh
   oregano
¼ cup chopped fresh
   parsley
2 tablespoons chopped
   fresh rosemary
2 tablespoons chopped
   fresh thyme
½ cup olive oil
½ cup balsamic vinegar

Combine oregano, parsley, rosemary, thyme, oil and vinegar in small bowl. Roast chicken according to rotisserie directions. Dip brush into herb mixture; brush chicken with herb mixture every 30 minutes for first 2 hours of roasting. Brush every 15 minutes during last hour of roasting.* Roast chicken until internal temperature reaches 180°F in thigh and meat is no longer pink.

Makes 16 servings

*Do not baste during last 5 minutes of roasting. Discard any remaining herb mixture.

Prep Time: 15 minutes plus roasting time

Magical Tip

To make an aromatic herb brush, bundle together sprigs of oregano, parsley, rosemary and thyme. Tie the bundle with kitchen string, then use it as a brush for spreading the pesto onto the chicken.

Rotisserie Chicken with Pesto Brush

Grilled Chicken Skewers

⅓ cup lemon juice

⅓ cup honey

1½ teaspoons LAWRY'S®
    Lemon Pepper

½ teaspoon LAWRY'S®
    Seasoned Salt

2 boneless, skinless
    chicken breast halves
    (about ½ pound), cut
    into thin strips

½ pound bacon slices
    Skewers

In large resealable plastic food storage bag, combine lemon juice, honey, Lemon Pepper and Seasoned Salt; mix well. Add chicken; seal bag. Marinate in refrigerator at least 30 minutes. Remove chicken; discard used marinade. Alternately thread chicken and bacon onto skewers. Grill or broil skewers 10 to 15 minutes or until chicken is no longer pink in center and juices run clear when cut, and bacon is crisp. *Makes 2 servings*

Serving Suggestions: Garnish with lemon wedges. Serve as a light entrée, or divide and serve as appetizers.

Hint: If using wooden skewers, soak in water overnight before using, to prevent scorching.

Grilled Chicken au Brie

1 (5-ounce) package
    ALOUETTE® Crème de
    Brie®

½ cup chopped walnuts,
    divided

4 slices bacon, cooked
    crisp and crumbled

2 tablespoons packed
    brown sugar

4 boneless skinless chicken
    breasts

Blend Crème de Brie, ¼ cup walnuts, bacon and brown sugar over low heat, stirring until mixture thins.

Grill or broil chicken until done.

Place chicken on individual serving dishes; ladle cheese sauce over chicken and sprinkle with remaining walnuts. *Makes 4 servings*

Grilled Chicken Skewers

Spicy Mango Chicken

¼ cup mango nectar

¼ cup chopped fresh
    cilantro

2 jalapeño chile peppers,*
    seeded and finely
    chopped

2 teaspoons LAWRY'S®
    Seasoned Salt

2 teaspoons vegetable oil

½ teaspoon LAWRY'S®
    Garlic Powder with
    Parsley

½ teaspoon ground cumin

4 boneless, skinless
    chicken breast halves
    (about 1 pound)

Mango & Black Bean
    Salsa (recipe follows)

*Jalapeño peppers can sting and irritate
the skin; wear rubber gloves when
handling peppers and do not touch eyes.

In small bowl, combine all ingredients except chicken and salsa; mix well. Brush marinade on both sides of chicken. Grill or broil chicken 10 to 15 minutes or until no longer pink in center and juices run clear when cut, turning once and basting often with additional marinade. *Do not baste during last 5 minutes of cooking.* Discard any remaining marinade. Top chicken with Mango & Black Bean Salsa.   *Makes 4 servings*

Mango & Black Bean Salsa

1 ripe mango, peeled, seeded and chopped

1 cup canned black beans, rinsed and drained

½ cup chopped tomato

2 thinly sliced green onions

1 tablespoon chopped fresh cilantro

1½ teaspoons lime juice

1½ teaspoons red wine vinegar

½ teaspoon LAWRY'S® Seasoned Salt

In medium bowl, combine all ingredients; mix well. Let stand 30 minutes to allow flavors to blend.

Makes about 2¾ cups

Spicy Mango Chicken

Hot 'n' Spicy Chicken Barbecue

½ cup A.1.® Steak Sauce
½ cup tomato sauce
¼ cup finely chopped onion
2 tablespoons cider
   vinegar
2 tablespoons maple syrup
1 tablespoon vegetable oil
2 teaspoons chili powder
½ teaspoon crushed red
   pepper flakes
1 (3-pound) chicken, cut up

Blend steak sauce, tomato sauce, onion, vinegar, maple syrup, oil, chili powder and red pepper flakes in medium saucepan. Heat mixture to a boil over medium heat; reduce heat. Simmer for 5 to 7 minutes or until thickened; cool.

Grill chicken over medium heat for 30 to 40 minutes or until done, turning and basting frequently with prepared sauce. Serve hot.   *Makes 4 servings*

Caribbean Jerk Chicken with Quick Fruit Salsa

1 cup plus 2 tablespoons
   LAWRY'S® Caribbean
   Jerk Marinade with
   Papaya Juice, divided
1 can (15¼ ounces)
   tropical fruit salad,
   drained
4 boneless, skinless
   chicken breast halves
   (about 1 pound)

In small glass bowl, combine 2 tablespoons Caribbean Jerk Marinade and tropical fruit; mix well and set aside. In large resealable plastic food storage bag, combine additional 1 cup Caribbean Jerk Marinade and chicken; seal bag. Marinate in refrigerator at least 30 minutes. Remove chicken from marinade; discard used marinade. Grill or broil chicken until no longer pink in center, about 10 to 15 minutes, turning halfway through grilling time. Top chicken with fruit salsa.

Makes 4 servings

Serving Suggestion: Serve with hot cooked rice and black beans.

Hot 'n' Spicy Chicken Barbecue

2½ **pounds chicken wings**
½ **cup** *Frank's® RedHot®* **Cayenne Pepper Sauce**
⅓ **cup butter or margarine, melted**
Prepared blue cheese salad dressing
Celery sticks

Cut off wing tips from chicken wings; discard. Cut wings in half between remaining joint to make two pieces. Place wing pieces on grid. Grill over medium-high coals 30 minutes or until thoroughly cooked and crispy, turning often. Place in large bowl.

Combine *Frank's RedHot* Sauce and butter. Pour over wings; toss well to coat evenly. Serve wings with blue cheese dressing and celery sticks.   *Makes 6 servings*

Shanghai Red Wings: Cook wings as directed. Combine ¼ cup soy sauce, 3 tablespoons *Frank's RedHot* Sauce, 3 tablespoons honey, 2 tablespoons peanut oil, 1 teaspoon grated peeled fresh ginger and 1 teaspoon minced garlic in small bowl; mix well. Pour over wings; toss well to coat evenly. Serve as directed.

Cajun Wings: Cook wings as directed. Combine ⅓ cup *Frank's RedHot* Sauce, ⅓ cup ketchup, ¼ cup (½ stick) melted butter or margarine and 2 teaspoons Cajun seasoning blend in small bowl; mix well. Pour over wings; toss well to coat evenly. Serve as directed.

Santa Fe Wings: Cook wings as directed. Combine ¼ cup *Frank's RedHot* Sauce, ¼ cup (½ stick) melted butter or margarine, ¼ cup chili sauce and 1 teaspoon chili powder in small bowl; mix well. Pour over wings; toss well to coat evenly. Serve as directed.

Prep Time: 10 minutes
Cook Time: 30 minutes

Oriental Grilled Chicken

½ cup soy sauce

¼ cup prepared mustard

2 tablespoons honey

2 tablespoons lemon juice

½ teaspoon ground ginger

4 chicken quarters

Hot cooked rice pilaf (optional)

Combine soy sauce, mustard, honey, lemon juice and ginger in large glass bowl. Add chicken, turning to coat. Cover; marinate in refrigerator 1 hour. Remove chicken. Place marinade in small saucepan. Bring to a boil over medium-high heat; keep warm. Place chicken on prepared grill, skin sides up, about 8 inches from heat. Grill, turning occasionally, 45 minutes. Grill, basting occasionally with marinade, 15 minutes more or until fork can be inserted into chicken with ease and juices run clear, not pink. Serve with hot rice pilaf.

Makes 4 servings

Favorite recipe from **National Chicken Council**

Barbecued "Bistro" Chicken

6 boneless chicken breast halves

½ cup KIKKOMAN® Teriyaki Baste & Glaze

2 tablespoons burgundy wine

2 cloves garlic, pressed

⅛ teaspoon pepper

Rinse chicken under cold water; pat dry with paper towels. Combine teriyaki baste & glaze, wine, garlic and pepper; set aside. Place chicken on grill 4 to 5 inches from hot coals. Cook 10 to 12 minutes, or until tender, turning over and brushing frequently with baste & glaze mixture during last 5 minutes of cooking time. (Or, place chicken on rack of broiler pan; brush with baste & glaze mixture. Broil 4 to 5 inches from heat 7 minutes on each side, or until tender, brushing occasionally with remaining baste & glaze mixture.)

Makes 6 servings

Glazed Chicken & Vegetable Skewers

12 small red or new
   potatoes, about
   1 ½ inches in diameter
   (1 pound)

Golden Glaze (recipe
   follows)

1 pound boneless skinless
   chicken thighs or
   breasts, cut into 1-inch
   pieces

1 yellow or red bell pepper,
   cut into 1-inch pieces

½ small red onion, cut into
   1-inch pieces

8 metal skewers (12 inches
   long)

Salt

1. Prepare grill for direct cooking.

2. Cook potatoes in boiling water until almost tender, about 10 minutes (or, microwave at HIGH 3 to 4 minutes or until almost tender). Rinse with cool water to stop the cooking.

3. Prepare Golden Glaze. Alternately thread chicken, potatoes, bell pepper and onion onto skewers. Brush glaze evenly over all sides of food.

4. Place skewers on grid over medium-hot coals. Grill, covered, 14 minutes for chicken breast or 16 minutes for chicken thighs, or until chicken is cooked through and vegetables are crisp-tender, turning once. Season to taste with salt.   *Makes 4 servings*

Final Prep and Cook Time: 25 to 30 minutes

Golden Glaze

¼ cup apricot or peach preserves
2 tablespoons spicy brown mustard*
2 cloves garlic, minced

*Dijon mustard may be substituted. Add ¼ teaspoon hot pepper sauce to glaze.

Combine all ingredients; mix well. Store tightly covered in refrigerator up to 2 weeks. (Marinade may easily be doubled for two uses.)   *Makes about ⅓ cup glaze*

Glazed Chicken & Vegetable Skewers

Grilled Rosemary Chicken

2 tablespoons lemon juice

2 tablespoons olive oil

2 cloves garlic, minced

2 tablespoons minced fresh rosemary

¼ teaspoon salt

4 boneless skinless chicken breasts

1. Whisk together lemon juice, oil, garlic, rosemary and salt in small bowl. Pour into shallow glass dish. Add chicken, turning to coat both sides with lemon juice mixture. Cover and marinate in refrigerator 15 minutes, turning chicken once.

2. Grill chicken over medium-hot coals 5 to 6 minutes per side or until chicken is no longer pink in center.

Makes 4 servings

Prep and Cook Time: 30 minutes

Italian Marinated Chicken

1 bottle (8 ounces) LAWRY'S® Herb & Garlic Marinade with Lemon Juice

2 tablespoons finely chopped onion

2 tablespoons lemon juice

¾ teaspoon LAWRY'S® Seasoned Pepper

6 boneless, skinless chicken breast halves (about 1½ pounds)

In large resealable plastic food storage bag, combine all ingredients except chicken; mix well. Add chicken to marinade; seal bag. Marinate in refrigerator at least 1 hour, turning occasionally. Remove chicken; discard used marinade. Grill or broil chicken 10 to 15 minutes or until no longer pink in center and juices run clear when cut.

Makes 6 to 8 servings

Serving Suggestion: Perfect served with any pasta or crisp green salad.

Hint: Chill leftover chicken and slice for use in salads or sandwiches.

Grilled Rosemary Chicken

Mediterranean Chicken Kabobs

Hot off the Grill

2 pounds boneless skinless chicken breasts or chicken tenders, cut into 1-inch pieces

1 small eggplant, peeled and cut into 1-inch pieces

1 medium zucchini, cut crosswise into ½-inch slices

2 medium onions, each cut into 8 wedges

16 medium mushrooms, stems removed

16 cherry tomatoes

1 cup fat-free reduced-sodium chicken broth

⅔ cup balsamic vinegar

3 tablespoons olive oil or vegetable oil

2 tablespoons dried mint leaves

4 teaspoons dried basil leaves

1 tablespoon dried oregano leaves

2 teaspoons grated lemon peel

Chopped fresh parsley (optional)

4 cups hot cooked couscous

1. Alternately thread chicken, eggplant, zucchini, onions, mushrooms and tomatoes onto 16 metal skewers; place in large glass baking dish.

2. Combine chicken broth, vinegar, oil, mint, basil and oregano in small bowl; pour over kabobs. Cover; marinate in refrigerator 2 hours, turning kabobs occasionally. Remove kabobs from marinade; discard marinade.

3. Grill kabobs on covered grill over medium-hot coals, 10 to 15 minutes or until chicken is no longer pink in center, turning kabobs halfway through cooking time. Or, broil kabobs 6 inches from heat source 10 to 15 minutes or until chicken is no longer pink in center, turning kabobs halfway through cooking time. Stir lemon peel and parsley, if desired, into couscous; serve with kabobs. *Makes 8 servings*

Magical Tip

Cleanup is easier if the grill rack is coated with vegetable oil or nonstick cooking spray before grilling.

Mediterranean Chicken Kabobs

Classic Grilled Chicken

1 whole frying chicken*
   (3½ pounds),
   quartered
¼ cup lemon juice
¼ cup olive oil
2 tablespoons soy sauce
2 large cloves garlic,
   minced
½ teaspoon sugar
½ teaspoon ground cumin
¼ teaspoon black pepper

*Substitute 3½ pounds chicken parts for whole chicken, if desired. Grill legs and thighs about 35 minutes and breast halves about 25 minutes or until chicken is no longer pink in center, turning once.

Rinse chicken under cold running water; pat dry with paper towels. Arrange chicken in 13×9×2-inch glass baking dish. Combine remaining ingredients in small bowl; pour half of mixture over chicken. Cover and reserve remaining mixture in refrigerator to use for basting. Cover and refrigerate chicken at least 1 hour or overnight. Remove chicken from marinade; discard marinade. Arrange medium KINGSFORD® Briquets on each side of large rectangular metal or foil drip pan. Pour hot tap water into drip pan until half full. Place chicken on grid directly above drip pan. Grill chicken, skin side down, on covered grill 25 minutes. Baste with reserved basting mixture. Turn chicken; cook 20 to 25 minutes or until juices run clear and chicken is no longer pink in center. *Makes 6 servings*

Magical Tip

Use long-handled tongs or a spatula to turn meat. A fork or knife punctures the meat and lets the juices escape.

Classic Grilled Chicken

Savory Chicken Satay

1 envelope LIPTON® RECIPE
    SECRETS® Onion Soup
    Mix

¼ cup olive or vegetable oil

2 tablespoons firmly
    packed brown sugar

2 tablespoons SKIPPY®
    Peanut Butter

1 pound boneless, skinless
    chicken breasts,
    pounded and cut into
    thin strips

12 to 16 wooden skewers,
    soaked in water

1. In large plastic bag, combine soup mix, oil, brown sugar and peanut butter. Add chicken and toss to coat well. Close bag and marinate in refrigerator 30 minutes.

2. Remove chicken from marinade; discard marinade. On large skewers, thread chicken, weaving back and forth.

3. Grill or broil chicken 8 minutes or until chicken is no longer pink in center. Serve with your favorite dipping sauces. *Makes 12 to 16 appetizers*

Prep Time: 15 minutes
Marinate Time: 30 minutes
Cook Time: 8 minutes

Magical Tip

Metal or bamboo skewers are used for kabobs, satays and appetizers. They are available in a variety of lengths. Select skewers that are flat rather than round, if possible, so the food will not slip around when the skewers are turned on the grill. Bamboo skewers, which are disposable, must be soaked in water 30 minutes before being used on a grill, to prevent them from burning.

Savory Chicken Satay

Barbecued Chicken

2½ to 3-pound broiler-fryer chicken, cut up

BARBECUE SAUCE

1 cup catsup

¼ cup GRANDMA'S® Molasses Unsulphured

¼ cup cider vinegar

¼ cup Dijon mustard

2 tablespoons Worcestershire sauce

1 teaspoon garlic powder

1 teaspoon hickory flavor liquid smoke

¼ teaspoon cayenne pepper

¼ teaspoon hot pepper sauce

In 12×8-inch (2-quart) microwave-safe baking dish, arrange chicken pieces with thickest portions to outside. In small bowl, combine all sauce ingredients; set aside.

Prepare barbecue grill. Cover chicken with waxed paper. Microwave on 100% (HIGH) for 10 minutes. Immediately place chicken on grill over medium heat. Brush with sauce. Cook 20 to 25 minutes or until no longer pink, turning once and brushing frequently with sauce.   *Makes 4 to 6 servings*

Note: This Barbecue Sauce is equally delicious on ribs.

Zesty Island Chicken Kabobs

2 boneless, skinless chicken breasts (about 8 ounces)

1 small orange, cut into wedges

¾ cup fresh or canned pineapple chunks

½ red bell pepper, cut into 1-inch pieces

½ green bell pepper, cut into 1-inch pieces

⅓ cup teriyaki sauce, divided

1 (2-cup) bag UNCLE BEN'S® Boil-in-Bag Rice

1. Cut chicken into 1-inch pieces. Thread chicken, orange, pineapple and red and green bell peppers alternately onto four 10-inch skewers. Brush some of teriyaki sauce over kabobs. Grill or broil kabobs 10 to 15 minutes or until chicken is no longer pink, turning once and brushing occasionally with remaining teriyaki sauce.

2. Meanwhile, prepare rice according to package directions. Serve kabobs over rice.   *Makes 2 servings*

Serving Suggestion: For a tropical touch, serve rice in a pineapple shell and top with kabobs.

Hot off the Grill

Lemon Fresh Chicken Grill

½ cup KIKKOMAN® Teriyaki
    Marinade & Sauce

1 tablespoon grated fresh
    lemon peel

2 tablespoons fresh lemon
    juice

½ teaspoon pepper

3 pounds frying chicken
    pieces

Combine teriyaki sauce, lemon peel, lemon juice and pepper; pour over chicken in large plastic food storage bag. Press air out of bag; close top securely. Refrigerate 8 hours or overnight, turning bag over occasionally. Reserving marinade, remove chicken; place on grill 5 to 6 inches from medium-hot coals. Cook 20 to 25 minutes on each side, or until chicken is no longer pink in center, brushing occasionally with reserved marinade during last 20 minutes of cooking time.* (Or, place chicken on rack of broiler pan. Broil 4 to 5 inches from heat 30 minutes, or until chicken is no longer pink in center, turning over and brushing occasionally with reserved marinade.*) *Makes 4 servings*

*Do not baste during last 5 minutes of cooking. Discard any remaining marinade.

Easy Grilled Chicken

⅔ cup white wine vinegar

⅔ cup water

3 tablespoons butter or
    margarine

2 tablespoons
    Worcestershire sauce

2 tablespoons garlic salt

1 tablespoon ground black
    pepper

4 chicken quarters

Combine vinegar, water, butter, Worcestershire, garlic salt and pepper in small saucepan. Bring to a boil over high heat. Brush sauce on chicken. Place chicken on prepared grill, skin sides up, about 8 inches from heat. Grill, turning and basting liberally with sauce every 5 to 10 minutes, about 60 to 70 minutes or until fork can be inserted into chicken with ease and juices run clear, not pink. Serve immediately. *Makes 4 servings*

Favorite recipe from **USA Rice Federation**

Southwest Chicken

2 tablespoons olive oil

1 clove garlic, pressed

1 teaspoon chili powder

1 teaspoon ground cumin

1 teaspoon dried oregano leaves

½ teaspoon salt

1 pound skinless boneless chicken breast halves or thighs

Combine oil, garlic, chili powder, cumin, oregano and salt; brush over both sides of chicken to coat. Grill chicken over medium-hot KINGSFORD® Briquets 8 to 10 minutes or until chicken is no longer pink, turning once. Serve immediately or use in Build a Burrito, Taco Salad or other favorite recipes. *Makes 4 servings*

Note: Southwest Chicken can be grilled ahead and refrigerated for several days or frozen for longer storage.

Build a Burrito: Top warm large flour tortillas with strips of Southwest Chicken and your choice of drained canned black beans, cooked brown or white rice, shredded cheese, salsa verde, shredded lettuce, sliced black olives and chopped cilantro. Fold in sides and roll to enclose filling. Heat in microwave oven at HIGH until heated through. (Or, wrap in foil and heat in preheated 350°F oven.)

Taco Salad: For a quick one-dish meal, layer strips of Southwest Chicken with tomato wedges, blue or traditional corn tortilla chips, sliced black olives, shredded romaine or iceberg lettuce, shredded cheese and avocado slices. Serve with salsa, sour cream, guacamole or a favorite dressing.

Taco Salad

Grilled Chicken, Rice & Veggies

3 ounces boneless skinless chicken breast

3 tablespoons reduced-fat Italian salad dressing, divided

½ cup fat-free reduced-sodium chicken broth

¼ cup uncooked rice

½ cup frozen broccoli and carrot blend, thawed

1. Place chicken and 1 tablespoon salad dressing in resealable plastic food storage bag. Seal bag; turn to coat. Marinate in refrigerator 1 hour.

2. Remove chicken from marinade; discard marinade. Grill chicken over medium-hot coals 8 to 10 minutes or until chicken is no longer pink in center.

3. Meanwhile, bring broth to a boil in small saucepan; add rice. Cover; reduce heat and simmer 15 minutes, stirring in vegetables during last 5 minutes of cooking. Remove from heat and stir in remaining 2 tablespoons dressing. Serve with chicken. *Makes 1 serving*

Magical Tip

To check the temperature of the coals, cautiously hold the palm of your hand at grid level—over the coals for direct heat and over the drip pan for indirect heat—and count the number of seconds you can hold your hand in that position before the heat forces you to pull it away. Use the following information as a guide:

2 Seconds: hot (about 375°F or more)
3 Seconds: medium-hot (about 350°F to 375°F)
4 Seconds: medium (about 300°F to 350°F)
5 Seconds: low (about 200°F to 300°F)

Grilled Chicken, Rice & Veggies

Wish-Bone® Marinade Italiano

¾ cup WISH-BONE® Italian
Dressing*

2½ to 3 pounds chicken
pieces**

*Also terrific with Wish-Bone® Robusto
Italian or Just 2 Good Italian Dressing.

**Or, use 6 boneless, skinless chicken
breast halves (about 1½ pounds).

In large, shallow nonaluminum baking dish or plastic
bag, pour ½ cup Italian dressing over chicken. Cover
dish or close bag, and marinate in refrigerator, turning
occasionally, 3 to 24 hours.

Remove chicken from marinade; discard marinade. Grill
or broil chicken, turning once and brushing frequently
with remaining dressing, until chicken is no longer
pink.   *Makes about 4 servings*

Grilled Summer Chicken & Vegetables

1¼ cups WISH-BONE® Italian
Dressing, divided*

4 chicken breast halves
(about 2 pounds)

4 ears fresh or frozen corn
(about 2 pounds)

2 large tomatoes, halved
crosswise

*Also terrific with WISH-BONE®
Robusto Italian or Lite Italian Dressing.

In large, shallow nonaluminum baking dish, pour 1 cup
Italian dressing over chicken, corn and tomatoes. Cover
and marinate chicken and vegetables in refrigerator,
turning occasionally, 3 to 24 hours.

Remove chicken and vegetables from marinade; discard
marinade. Grill or broil chicken and corn 20 minutes,
turning and brushing frequently with remaining
dressing. Arrange tomato halves, cut sides up, on grill or
broiler pan and continue cooking chicken and
vegetables, turning and brushing occasionally with
dressing, 10 minutes or until chicken is no longer pink
and corn is tender.   *Makes 4 servings*

Wish-Bone® Marinade Italiano

Acknowledgments

The publisher would like to thank the companies and organizations listed below for the use of their recipes and photographs in this publication.

A.1.® Steak Sauce

BC-USA, Inc.

Birds Eye®

Bob Evans®

Butterball® Turkey Company

Chef Paul Prudhomme's Magic Seasoning Blends®

ConAgra Grocery Products Company

Del Monte Corporation

Dole Food Company, Inc.

Egg Beaters®

Grandma's® is a registered trademark of Mott's, Inc.

Guiltless Gourmet®

Holland House® is a registered trademark of Mott's, Inc.

Kikkoman International Inc.

Kraft Foods Holdings

Lawry's® Foods, Inc.

Mushroom Council

National Chicken Council / US Poultry & Egg Association

Perdue Farms Incorporated

PLANTERS® Nuts

Reckitt Benckiser

Riviana Foods Inc.

The Golden Grain Company®

The Hidden Valley® Food Products Company

The J.M. Smucker Company

The Kingsford Products Company

Tyson Foods, Inc.

Uncle Ben's Inc.

Unilever Bestfoods North America

USA Rice Federation

Wisconsin Milk Marketing Board

Index

Index

METRIC CONVERSION CHART

VOLUME MEASUREMENTS (dry)

$\frac{1}{8}$ teaspoon = 0.5 mL
$\frac{1}{4}$ teaspoon = 1 mL
$\frac{1}{2}$ teaspoon = 2 mL
$\frac{3}{4}$ teaspoon = 4 mL
1 teaspoon = 5 mL
1 tablespoon = 15 mL
2 tablespoons = 30 mL
$\frac{1}{4}$ cup = 60 mL
$\frac{1}{3}$ cup = 75 mL
$\frac{1}{2}$ cup = 125 mL
$\frac{2}{3}$ cup = 150 mL
$\frac{3}{4}$ cup = 175 mL
1 cup = 250 mL
2 cups = 1 pint = 500 mL
3 cups = 750 mL
4 cups = 1 quart = 1 L

VOLUME MEASUREMENTS (fluid)

1 fluid ounce (2 tablespoons) = 30 mL
4 fluid ounces ($\frac{1}{2}$ cup) = 125 mL
8 fluid ounces (1 cup) = 250 mL
12 fluid ounces ($1\frac{1}{2}$ cups) = 375 mL
16 fluid ounces (2 cups) = 500 mL

WEIGHTS (mass)

$\frac{1}{2}$ ounce = 15 g
1 ounce = 30 g
3 ounces = 90 g
4 ounces = 120 g
8 ounces = 225 g
10 ounces = 285 g
12 ounces = 360 g
16 ounces = 1 pound = 450 g

DIMENSIONS

$\frac{1}{16}$ inch = 2 mm
$\frac{1}{8}$ inch = 3 mm
$\frac{1}{4}$ inch = 6 mm
$\frac{1}{2}$ inch = 1.5 cm
$\frac{3}{4}$ inch = 2 cm
1 inch = 2.5 cm

OVEN TEMPERATURES

250°F = 120°C
275°F = 140°C
300°F = 150°C
325°F = 160°C
350°F = 180°C
375°F = 190°C
400°F = 200°C
425°F = 220°C
450°F = 230°C

BAKING PAN SIZES

Utensil	Size in Inches/Quarts	Metric Volume	Size in Centimeters
Baking or Cake Pan (square or rectangular)	8×8×2	2 L	20×20×5
	9×9×2	2.5 L	23×23×5
	12×8×2	3 L	30×20×5
	13×9×2	3.5 L	33×23×5
Loaf Pan	8×4×3	1.5 L	20×10×7
	9×5×3	2 L	23×13×7
Round Layer Cake Pan	8×1½	1.2 L	20×4
	9×1½	1.5 L	23×4
Pie Plate	8×1¼	750 mL	20×3
	9×1¼	1 L	23×3
Baking Dish or Casserole	1 quart	1 L	—
	1½ quart	1.5 L	—
	2 quart	2 L	—